BALLS

How to Keep Your
Relationship Alive
When You Live with a
Sports-Obsessed Guy

By Ernestine Sclafani Bayless

WITH SKIP BAYLESS

D0067796

Dedication

I dedicate this book to my mother, Evelyn Jacobs.

She believed in me more than I believed in myself.

We were more than mother and daughter: we were best friends. We could talk about anything and everything—no topic was off limits. She was there for me 24/7 and would always remind me that "There is no one better than you."

Without her constant love, support, and magical NYC stories, I would not be the woman I am today.

She taught me what the term "unconditional love" means.

She passed on to me a special quality that lived inside of her. Some would call it self-confidence, but my Jewish mother called it "chutzpah."

Mom, I may not have you physically by my side anymore, but I hold you in my heart, my soul, and my thoughts every minute of the day. And guess what? I still have chutzpah!

I love you more than life itself.

Contents

Acknowledgments

There are certain people who have stuck by me through thick and thin, so here it goes:

First off, Skip Bayless, a man with whom I believe God broke the mold when he was born. He is one of the most unique and special men I have ever met. His love, kindness, loyalty, dedication, spirituality, sense of humor, and amazing mind make me love him more and more each day that passes and we are together. As he knows, from the moment we met, our lives were never going to be the same. And I wouldn't want it any other way! I love you more.

My sister, Joyce, who without her friendship, love, and sense of humor, we could not have climbed all those countless hills and mountains together that life threw our way! In the end, we can still sit back and laugh at it all. Love you, Sis.

My best friend, Francesca, aka "Pallie," we were destined to be best friends! Lucy dancing with Van, Ann Marie's flip, those adorable pedal pushers, *Sunday in New York*, and Christmas snow globes. Need I say more?

Karen O, my past and present friend. They say what goes around comes around. Well, our friendship has made the complete circle, and now that circle will never be broken!

Laura F, you started out as my MD, but a friendship blossomed, and now we are pals. No prescription you could ever write could provide all the wonderful moments we have had as friends!

Patty N, our friendship began at GMA, continued through Bally, Edelman, Weber, East Coast, West Coast . . . no matter where life takes us, we will always remain gal pals!

Fran K, we've had numerous "deep life talks" as we walk through Central Park, but somehow we always end up laughing by the time we hit Fifth Avenue. We've also sat behind countless big-headed people with colds at Broadway shows, but we always end up chuckling at that as well. True friends can find laughter together no matter where they are, and that's us.

Tom BB, the world is spinning. We are in it and still going strong! You and I will always have the St. Regis. XO.

Corinne F, if you weren't a lawyer, you could have been a professional cheerleader. You have been rooting for me since the first day we met, and I adore you for that!

Chris Fahey, you are a special lady with one of the biggest hearts I know. You are also one of the nicest things that came out of my PR work life.

Nachamie, what would I do without your funny emails, quick wit, incredible knowledge, friendship, and love you have bestowed upon me for the last 20-something years.

John G, you are my only friend who calls me "Ern," has won a Tony, was a Jeopardy question, and never ages. I cherish the day we met.

Ayala, you are a sweet and caring friend who always has the ability to "make sense" when it comes to love.

Craig (Doc), all roads lead to DC; he is the reason you and I became friends. I know there is a higher power. XO.

DC, thin-crust Domino's (it's like a matzo!), Sharon's Sorbet (how can this be 100 calories?), Tony Bennett's *Steppin' Out*, chocolate-covered pretzels, and Lucky Kentucky Shampoo. Godspeed, Mamaleh.

And to My LA Pals

Dr. K, you are my eye saver, my good friend, and one of the coolest and hippest people I know. You were one of the first people who helped make my NY to LA life more fun, just by knowing you.

Laura F, I never knew there were so many hip rooftop dining spots in LA! You are one super woman. Thanks for sharing your Saturday afternoons with me, which are always filled with laughs and the best girl talk this side of Wilshire Boulevard.

Andrea, I never thought I would find a friend who knows more about old Hollywood stars than I do. You are a real "doozy."

Deborah Lynn, my sweet friend who will forever be a Southern California flower-power hippie chick filled with love, peace, rainbows, and sunshine. Love ya!

Doug and Amy, There is only one word that describes the two of you: AWESOME. I am proud to call you both my friends and flattered to be an honorary "O" cuz!

Eva B, You are one BADASS workout warrior. You get my blood pumping and heart racing at 6 a.m., and I always come back for more. I think it's for the fun laughs and stories in between the sweating.

Introduction

If your man is crazed about sports—if you think he cares more about what game is on than about your relationship—I'm here to help. As you'll see in the pages ahead, no matter how sports-obsessed your guy is, he doesn't come close to my Skip.

For much of my life, the closest I ever came to a football game was playing clarinet in my high-school marching band. I grew up on Long Island and in Manhattan, but the only Jets I knew took me from JFK to Hawaii, and the only Giants I ever read about were in "Jack and the Beanstalk."

Before I met Skip I did showroom sales for Izod Lacoste sportswear for ten years. I then became a vice president in the media division for Weber Shandwick. The occasional passerby mistook me for Sarah Jessica Parker, and I sometimes felt I was living a real-life episode of *Sex and the City* meets *I Love Lucy*. I dated several actors and singers—all non-athletic—capped off by one very famous entertainer who did watch the Yankees and this weird sports show called *Cold Pizza*. Two guys debated each other about sports—one guy he loved and the other, according to my special man, was an idiot. Little did I know I would eventually marry the idiot.

Pre-Skip, my evenings were filled with concerts, movies, and theater. Now that Skip and I are married, my entire life revolves around watching games—sometimes four or five a day, three or four a night. College and pro football games. College and pro basketball games, men and women. Baseball games. Soccer games. Women's college softball games. Little League World Series. Tennis matches. Golf tournaments. Auto racing. Hockey. Even boxing—yes, I sit with one or both eyes closed "watching" the sport I despise most.

My life has come to this: I can call offensive fouls in a televised NBA basketball game before the ref does. ("That's a charge!") I can yell at the TV screen while watching an NFL game. ("That's a horse collar!") I can name just about every San Antonio Spur, tell you Tom Brady's life story, and feel like I grew up with Adrian Peterson.

Now my life pretty much IS sports. That's because I'm married to a man whose very existence revolves around watching, following, and obsessing 24 hours a day over sports, sports, sports, and more sports. His name is Skip Bayless, and on our first date in 2005, he told me that his job is his life.

He debates sports for two and a half hours daily on *Undisputed*, the show he drives on Fox Sports 1 in Los Angeles. For 12 years, he lived the same life in New York and Connecticut doing similar work on ESPN, first on *Cold Pizza* and then the ratings juggernaut *First Take*. I have successfully found a place in that life since his second year on ESPN when I brought the actor Kevin Dillon to appear on *Cold Pizza*. (More on that billion-to-one moment later.)

My husband, love him or hate him, has become the most powerful voice in sports media. The astounding irony is that while thousands of guys of all team colors and ages would crawl to Los Angeles to get to watch one game with my husband, I've learned to *force* myself to watch tons of games with him, just so we can spend some "couple time" together.

This book is about how I have kept my relationship alive—and still going strong—while learning how to coexist with his "other woman" I've come to know, live with, and put a name to: sports.

Understand, the saving grace of our relationship is two-fold, I do my best to sit next to Skip and really try to understand games, and he wants to be with me when he isn't prepping for his show or living and nearly dying while watching games he has picked on national TV. Our marriage works because we do everything we can to be present in each other's lives: we work around each other's schedules, and we are open and flexible, all in the name of love.

It's likely your man isn't quite as crazed about sports as mine is—after all, it's Skip's job. But because of my extreme version of your life, I think I can help you better understand how to stay in love with him even when he's in love with sports. I will share my secrets, tricks, methods, and ways of maintaining my sanity.

You are not alone in this. Every time you think you have it bad with your sports-mad guy, know that I have it worse. Know that I'm making it work.

Early on in my relationship with Skip, my mother asked me this: "Would you rather he went to Hooters to watch games with the guys?"

Obviously not.

"Then figure out how to watch games with him."

Then she asked an even bigger question: "Is he worth it?"

Yes, he is.

"Then learn to watch sports."

Chapter 1

How I Met Skip

Through my childhood, sports were as foreign to me as Transylvania. I grew up out on Long Island near the Hamptons in middle-class Mastic Beach, a two-hour drive from Manhattan. I was the youngest, mommy's little girl. I think my brother played some organized soccer, but my sister, eight years older than me, was strictly interested in guys, dance clubs, sports cars, and '60s rock and roll. My father, a Sicilian, came from Mott Street in Manhattan's Little Italy. He had zero interest in National Football League games—he preferred we learned about the world watching *National Geographic*. He pushed us to learn about classical music, ballet, and painting—anything but sports. He was an engineer who was up at 4 a.m. and didn't get home until 7 p.m. His hobbies were photography and working on our cars.

My mom, Jewish, came from the Lower East Side of Manhattan. She was once a hatcheck girl at Dreamland Dance Hall and would tell me glamorous stories about seeing stars like Frank Sinatra and Tony Bennett hanging out in her nightclub. I vowed to myself that one day, I would live, work, and make it big in the City That Never Sleeps.

By the way, the one and only game my mom played was poker with guy friends from the neighborhood—regularly, as in several times a week. That was Evelyn Jacobs Sclafani: a beautiful blend of a die-for-her-kids Jewish mother and her own woman, tough as any man. Growing up poor fighting anti-Semitism will do that to a New York woman. She loved going to Atlantic City to play blackjack. She even dared to defy the unwritten rules of her family and faith by running away and marrying an Italian man and moving to the suburbs to start and raise a family. For my mother's parents, it wasn't kosher to bring home a "goyim." She married the Italian when she was 18.

All went reasonably well for nearly the first 40 years of their marriage. Then he found another woman, my mother wouldn't stand for it, and they began to fight so furiously that I began to fear for my mother's safety. Sicilian temper vs. Jewish I-won't-stand-for-that. It got so bad that he wanted us gone, and I wanted my mother out of the house. So, for a while, we left. This convinced me more than ever that I belonged in New York City.

My role model was Marlo Thomas in the groundbreaking TV show *That Girl*. She played Ann Marie, an aspiring actress and model trying to make it BY HERSELF AND ON HER OWN in NYC. She never seemed to have much of a job, but her clothes and her apartment were to die for. I wanted to be Ann Marie: independent, sassy, sexy, beautiful, smart, and willing to try just about any kooky scheme to get ahead. I also loved *I Love Lucy*. Ann Marie was Lucy Ricardo without Ricky, Fred, Ethel, and little Ricky. Ann Marie had a boyfriend named Donald Hollinger who was . . . drum roll . . . a writer who at times covered SPORTS!

Little did I know at the time I shared Ann Marie's destiny in more ways than one. Me, winding up with a sports writer? Ha ha. Fat chance. No way.

I moved from Long Island into a women's hotel in Greenwich Village run by The Salvation Army called The Markle Residence. My first job was working for Izod Lacoste on Seventh Avenue and 36th Street, in the heart of the Garment Center. I was the assistant to Jack McKenna, who was president of the company's accessories division. He was a sweet middle-aged man who was an excellent golfer and knew just about every sports star, athlete, and celebrity in the world. On any given day, the glass door to our showroom would open and in would walk Bucky Dent, Leroy Neiman, Arnold Palmer, Kirk Douglas, Johnny Carson . . . the list would go on and on. I recognized the Hollywood stars but not the athletes. I was clueless as to the magnitude of their popularity.

Later, when I was working for Bally of Switzerland, I read a story in which Mike Piazza—then a catcher for the Los Angeles Dodgers, soon to be acquired by the New York Mets—wore our shoes. So I cold-called his manager, who connected me with Mike, who hit it off with me. Maybe it helped that my father was Italian. Maybe it also helped that I have a healthy dose of my mother's irresistible charisma (guys were always charmed by her wherever she went). Mike and I didn't date—he was seven years younger than me. We just became friends and confidants. He would ask my advice on various starlets he was dating. I was a good listener.

Sometimes he would pick me up for lunch at my showroom. My coworkers would be astounded as I would leave arm-in-arm with MIKE PIAZZA—and boy, those arms were huge. But what's astoundingly ironic and true was that I barely knew who he was as a baseball star and that we never, ever discussed baseball.

I have always been attracted to guys without "normal" jobs—musicians, actors, performers, entertainers, and creative types in general. The longer the hair, the better.

Which brings me to my very special guy. He was an extremely talented actor, singer, and Broadway star, who also happened to be a teen heartthrob years earlier on a highly-rated TV show.

Just about every girl my age wanted to date and marry this baby-faced, shaggy, long-haired sex symbol. Through my teenage years, I had a poster of him hanging on my bedroom wall in Mastic Beach. He had a scar that was visible on the poster, and each night before I went to sleep, I kissed the scar. Even now, I'm not embarrassed to write that line.

My fantasy would eventually become a 12-year reality. Even crazier, my "teen idol" would ultimately "introduce" me to Skip Bayless. Go figure.

I met him while he was on Broadway and I was still at Bally of Switzerland. I had worked with many costumers in TV and theater, providing product for their show; in return, they would list my company's name in their playbill or show credits. I had invited a few of the show's cast, including "him," to my showroom. The guys were wearing Bally in their show, so I thought perhaps they would want to wear Bally in real life. Obviously, product on a celebrity is a major score for a PR person.

He ended up being one of the nicest guys ever, and we clicked as if we had known each other forever.

He was no longer that heartthrob I dreamed about; he was my real-life boyfriend.

He was separated from his wife, and they had a very young son. His estranged wife split her time between Los Angeles and New York City, enabling him to spend as much time as possible with the boy.

He was a sports fan; he especially loved the Yankees and this weird sports show called *Cold Pizza*. One day, he was at my place watching the show when I walked through the living room and asked him what the premise was. He said two guys debated each other about sports: one guy he loved and the other one, according to my boyfriend, was an idiot. I took one look at the TV, and all I could think was, "Wow, the one he doesn't like is actually kind of cute."

I didn't know it then, but I would eventually marry "the idiot."

My job was to strategize with teams, and in addition, book clients' spokespeople on various media outlets that would let them promote their products with a mention during the interview. Two weeks after my introduction to *Cold Pizza*, I booked actor Kevin Dillon (during the height of his *Entourage* popularity) to appear on several New York morning shows, the last stop being *Cold Pizza*. I knew so little about sports that I still didn't connect Skip with the show. But I did call my mother and say, "Well, it's a guy's sports show, so maybe I should wear a short dress and high heels. Maybe I'll meet someone." (At this point, I was feeling lost and confused in my relationship with my heartthrob. I loved him, but I also knew it was time to re-evaluate what I had and where it was going.)

So on that fateful day, I accompanied Kevin Dillon to his shows and ended up in the *Cold Pizza* green room while he went out on set. My clients were from Hanes sportswear—that's what Kevin would promote on air: the tagless T-shirt—and the two women from Hanes mentioned "how cute that Skip Bayless is." That's when it clicked for me: "Oh, yeah, this is the guy we were watching in my living room."

In a bizarre event that had never happened before and hasn't happened since, Skip had forgotten his notes for his final debate of the show that day. During the commercial break, he had to make a mad dash from the studio to his dressing room to retrieve the notes. He literally ran past the door of the green room, where we caught each other's eyes. I guess I gave him a look of familiarity because he stopped and said, "Do I know you?"

"I'm Ernestine," I said.

He later confided that he wasn't sure what to say—he gets possessed during his show, just lost in how to win the next live TV debate. So now neither of us was thinking clearly.

He asked where I lived. I said, "51st and Second." I actually lived at 52nd and First. Even as I was answering, I was thinking, "Girl, you're giving him the wrong streets." Then I handed him my card and said, "If you ever need anything in PR . . ." And he literally took off running.

My coworker Katie, who was with me in the green room, immediately turned to me and said, "You're going to marry him." I laughed and said, "You are nuts!"

I left Kevin after the show and called my mom and sister before my feet hit Eighth Avenue. "I met this guy, and he's cute." Then I walked over to my best friend Francesca's office—Francesca Fusco is one of the country's leading dermatologists in a practice with a prominent celebrity clientele. As any BFF would immediately ask, "Married? Single? Straight? Gay?" I said, "I have no idea. All I know is that he's on a sports show and seems nice."

Looking back, we were focusing on the wrong issues. What Francesca should have asked me was this: "Can you live with a man whose entire life is based on watching sports?"

In true New York, *Sex and the City* fashion, I did wonder how a guy this good-looking on a successful sports show would be single. I also thought, "There has to be something wrong with him." But what was "wrong" with him was like nothing I could have ever imagined.

I later found out Skip had left a long-term relationship when he moved from San Francisco to New York a year earlier. He was so driven to make his new morning show a success that he hadn't had a single date in an entire year. He had to be up by 3 a.m. every weekday morning—a social-life killer—and he was also writing columns for ESPN. com in the afternoons. So he was happily living in his sports bubble and not looking to meet anyone—especially a woman who never watched sports. *But* . . . that night he *did* send me an email saying it was nice meeting me and apologizing for having to run so quickly.

He now says, "Even though we talked for less than a minute, I was immediately physically attracted to you—and the bonus was your amazing personality—and I was in such a rush I feared I came off like a real 'TV star' jerk. There was just something about you . . . I felt an immediate click, and I wasn't even looking to get back into a relationship. Then, that night just happened to be a rare Friday night when I didn't have any sports I had to watch, so I had a little free time to think about whether I should email you or not."

No sports to watch? Now THAT was an upset. But there was something about the email he sent that somehow signaled to me there could be something here. I had become increasingly frustrated with my current relationship. I had considered breaking up with him for quite a while, but I just didn't have the heart or nerve to follow through with it. The connection we shared was so strong that the thought of ending it made me sick to my stomach.

You might call that first, billion-to-one, less-than-a-minute conversation with Skip love at first fright. It scared me into action. My intuition told me it was time to face the fact I had just turned 43 and couldn't spend the rest of my life chasing after the poster on my wall—especially when the real-life poster guy had made it painfully and relentlessly clear he was in no hurry to file for divorce. He was afraid the divorce would take a toll on his son, just like his parent's divorce took a toll on him when he was five years old. It shook me into reality that there just might be life after my teen idol, and maybe even a better life than what I'd had for 12 years with him. I loved him, but I did not love our life together, which seemed to be not moving forward.

I angsted for over a week and, boom, I decided to break up with him. There are times in your life when you make a decision that you just know is right and there's no second-guessing it. You just do it and never look back. This was one of those moments.

I called him, and within three minutes, a 12-year relationship I thought would never end was over. I had no real idea whether one quick, awkward conversation with Skip and one email from him would ever amount to anything. But something inside of me said breaking up was what I had to do. I went cold turkey. He asked if we could still be friends. I thought about it for a second and said no. He called me numerous times asking to see me, but I decided the past was the past.

I always listen to my gut.

Skip and I began a two-week email relationship, during which we somehow concocted some nutty scenario in which we had been together for years and now were divorcing—but who was getting custody of our dog, Spotty? We at least had email chemistry. But no calls. I began to wonder if something was fishy here. I asked my mother, my sister, and Francesca if they thought what I thought: was he married? Was he just out for some online fun while his wife was in the other room?

I plunged. I called the *Cold Pizza* office, got his voice mail, and left him a message. What was the worst that could happen? If he didn't return my call, well, then I could pull the plug on an ongoing email relationship I was beginning to grow weary of. I left a funny message saying that I needed to see him so I could hand Spotty over to him for the weekend.

Another trillion-to-one shot: Skip swears he never checked his voicemail the entire time he was at *Cold Pizza*. He had made plans to go to a movie with a female coworker who was just a friend—they were "movie buddies" and had seen eight or 10 films together through his first year on the show. But that Friday night, she canceled at the last second. For some fateful reason, he decided to check his voicemail.

Meant to be.

Suddenly, an email popped up on my computer screen from Skip saying he'd be home all evening if I wanted to talk, and he gave me his number. So I called him. We ended up staying on the phone for over two hours. He was half watching a Yankees game but said it wasn't that big a deal. He would comment occasionally on something that happened in the game, but I didn't think much of it. "It's his job," I thought. I even turned on the game so I could be aware of commercial breaks and know when I had his full attention. Only later did I realize I'd been given a preview of my next life.

During our chat, I found out that he—what!?—loved *I Love Lucy* and knew every episode. *Lucy* is my all-time favorite show—I can recite every famous line from every famous episode and know every episode verbatim. And—you're kidding!?—he also loved Woody Allen movies, my other favorite.

Home run (for me, not the Yankees).

Skip was funny, nice, spiritual, respectful, and not married, and he didn't have a girlfriend. He came from the opposite end of the earth from me—Oklahoma City—and soon pointed out that they no longer traveled by covered wagon in his hometown. I told him my mother was Jewish and my father was Italian, but neither had pushed me in any religious direction—Judaism or Catholicism. Skip later asked if I'd go to his Methodist church with him; now I've been going with him for

12 years. So how we worshiped wasn't an issue. But what he worshiped every night soon would be.

During our first phone conversation, I thought, "What's a little sports?"

I had NO CLUE.

We had our first date the next night. He met me outside my apartment building (I had to tell him I went dyslexic during that first frantic greenroom conversation: I lived at 52nd and First, not 51st and Second). We decided—since we both love pizza—we would walk down to a little place on First Avenue that makes the best whole-wheat pizza in New York. We each got a slice. As we ate, I was curious if he liked to date women who know a lot about sports. He told me it didn't matter. He said, "I talk sports all day and watch sports at night, so it's refreshing to be around someone who doesn't need to talk about sports."

The truth was, he didn't have a clue, either.

I told him I'd been to only one professional game in my entire life—a Yankees game with my actor friend Giancarlo Esposito, who brought along Susan Sarandon's 10-year-old son, Miles. We sat right behind the dugout. I remember only that the popcorn was good and that Miles had sushi at a baseball game. Skip suggested that one day, maybe, we would go—but that sitting in the stands was always difficult for him because fans would ask his thoughts throughout the game, making it tough for his own watching. After 12 years, we still haven't attended a game together—he has just become too recognizable and too controversial. But I have watched all or parts of 50,000 televised games with him.

The last thing Skip told me before he walked away from our date was a painful truth. I appreciated it and was offended by it all at once. He said, "Just to be fair to you, I'm going to be honest up front. If this relationship goes anywhere, please remember that you will always be No. 2 to my work. It's just the way I've always been." After that statement, I thought, "Who cares? I'm not marrying him!" Surprise!

The relationship/marriage-saving truth is that Skip soon made me No. 1, right next to his work. So it's Ernestine No. 1, his work No. 1-A. And, between you and me, I usually take priority over his work. That, I

can live with. Unless, of course, it's the Super Bowl, World Series, NBA Finals . . .

With our first date coming to a close, we awkwardly kissed goodnight—a peck on the lips. Then he even more awkwardly announced to me, "As crazy as this might sound, they've given me Sunday and Monday [Labor Day] off before football season starts, when I'll be pretty much working seven days a week. We're even taking our show to college game sites all over the country every Friday. So if we have any shot at getting to know each other, it has to be tomorrow and Monday."

We tripped the light fantastic for the next 48 hours and found we had so much in common—we loved the same movies, eating healthy and staying fit, and walking all over New York instead of taking cabs or subways. I quickly decided this was a guy I could really like.

Then real life kicked back in. "Kicked" as in football.

Every Thursday after his show, he flew off to some remote college town—Blacksburg, Virginia; Tuscaloosa, Alabama; or South Bend, Indiana. He usually got back too late on Friday night for us to do much.

Then College Football Saturday started happening. Every Saturday in the fall, he started watching at noon Eastern time. At first, I thought, "Well, this will be over by 3 p.m. or so." He grew up a crazed University of Oklahoma fan, so it always seemed like the noon game was his Sooners vs. Kansas, or Wyoming, or Rhode Island, or somebody. But then in the second half, he would start watching Notre Dame on his second TV while he was watching his Sooners.

I would say, "Who are we rooting for?" He'd say, "The guys in red, not the guys in blue." Then I'd go to the bathroom, come back, and find the colors had changed. Just as I got to know who the red guy was, he would change the game. He was now focused on a team in green "outfits" vs. one in black "outfits." (He got a kick out of my using a fashion term, yet constantly corrected me with, "No, they're uniforms.") By early evening, we were watching Alabama or Tennessee or Florida— and maybe on the second TV, his alma mater Vanderbilt, featuring this quarterback he loved named Jay Cutler. I can now tell you Jay Cutler's life story (BTW, this was way before he married TV star Kristin Cavallari) even though Skip finally had to give up defending him on his show.

Finally, around 10:30 p.m., YET ANOTHER GAME started and went seemingly endlessly until around 2 a.m.—usually it was USC featuring coach Pete Carroll, an ageless frat-boy type in his mid-50s running crazy up and down the sideline chewing his gum to beat the band. Pete Carroll was scruffy and good-looking with the longish gray hair and five o'clock shadow of an older surfer with a younger body. Pete Carroll was sexy. Unlike so many stuffy, arch-conservative "dad" or "granddad" coaches, Pete Carroll coached in a USC sweatshirt. I could watch Pete Carroll. If USC was the last game of the day, I could hang in with Pete Carroll until 2 a.m. But what a way to spend an "off" day and a Saturday night with the new love of my life.

Yet it is crucial to point out that Skip never expected or demanded that I watch games with him. He would've been completely content watching them by himself. Not once has he ever complained about not being able to watch with guy friends or coworkers. Not once has he ever complained about anything else I wanted to do with any of my friends while he was watching his games. He was happy if I wanted to watch or not watch. It was clear from that first date we were extremely compatible—he always says there's no one else in the world he'd rather spend time with than me, and I feel the same. We are constantly together. We don't need breaks from each other. In that way, our relationship has been one long fairy tale.

It's just that his job is so time-consuming that I realized pretty quickly that, if I wanted to see him at all, I would have to watch games with him. Sharing his game-watching space was a big challenge. But if I couldn't do it, I wasn't sure this relationship was going to survive.

Also, please appreciate this: My tolerance for game watching didn't happen overnight. I was highly concerned about whether or not I could be involved with a guy who lived for sports, not only for his work, but in his free time as well. I swore when I rented my first apartment, after my stint in the woman's hotel, that I would never give up having my own place, even if I married and lived in a different apartment with my man. I ended up keeping my apartment for the first 10 years of our relationship. Maybe it was the *That Girl* in me. I'm a combination of fiercely independent single girl—refusing to rely on a guy to take care of me financially or emotionally—and a fiercely loyal and dedicated lover and wife—willing to sacrifice to make a marriage work because this guy is worth it.

Skip and I didn't get married for the first 11 years of our relationship. We were engaged in 2010 but had no plans of tying the knot as most couples do within a year. We never felt the pressure or urge. We felt we were married already, just without the paperwork. During the week, he worked at ESPN about two hours by car away from New York City, where I worked. We saw each other every weekend—either he would come back to New York or I would go up to Bristol, Connecticut. But when he took a job in Los Angeles to start a new show on Fox Sports 1, that was it. Fish or cut bait. Marriage or bust. I insisted we get married. Skip agreed and felt the same way. I was not going to move to another state away from a place I called home, friends I loved, and a job I'd had for the last 12 years without a real marriage license in hand.

So we did it. We were married at City Hall on July 28, 2016, and we moved to LA on August 1, 2016. Me, a New York City girl, living near the Fox Studios in West LA? Even as I write this, I still can't believe it! And just for the record, I have my bagels from Essa Bagels, and knishes from Yonah Schimmel, both FedExed every few weeks. (If only Ray's Pizza on Eighth and 53rd would deliver!)

Today, Skip is even more obsessed with his job. His show has expanded from two hours live to two and a half. Here, he has to be up at 2 a.m., which was always 5 in Bristol. (I too am up before the rooster crows.) Here, Skip has his watch set to NY time (and so do I), and I will swear he watches even more sports than ever.

And often, I watch with him. This is my story of how an anti-sports girl learned to live with the ultimate sports guy, with advice about how you can live happily ever after with your sports guy.

Chapter 2

How Skip Met Me

Of course, every great story has two sides to it. Here's how Skip tells it.

The key to any marital or long-term relationship is connection. In my experience, relationships built solely on physical attraction are almost always doomed to fail. Relationships built solely on financial attraction often become empty and troubled. The key question is this: Do you love spending time with your spouse or partner—as in, are you happy taking long drives together, just the two of you? Or would that be your worst nightmare?

After 14 years together, the main reason Ernestine and I are still going strong—OK, some days, it's more like hanging in—is that not once have I ever been bored with her. NOT ONCE. Not once have I dreaded having to spend an evening with her. Not once have I tried making an excuse to get out of having to see her so I could do something with the guys or even just spend some time alone. I always have fun with her, even if we're just watching a bad movie or talking about how much we've spoiled Hazel, our Maltese, beyond repair. Ernestine is by far my best friend.

She has told the story about how we met. Here's my version and what it meant to me.

I had been out of a long-term relationship for about a year and was not looking to date anyone. I was doing just fine by myself. But that fateful morning at my show *Cold Pizza*, which we did live every morning in a studio beneath the New Yorker Hotel at 34th and Eighth, I left my notes for our final segment in my dressing room. I had never done that, and I haven't done that since. As I literally ran down the hall during a commercial break, I glanced sideways into the green room and caught the gaze of a woman I'd never seen before.

"Hi," she said and waved. Which brought me to a sudden halt, clock ticking.

"Do I know you?" I asked.

"I'm Ernestine," she said. Yes, she was.

We chatted awkwardly for maybe 45 seconds, and she gave me her card. You might call it love at first spark. There was just something startling to me about the way we instantly clicked.

We exchanged emails over the next couple of weeks, but I can't say I was thinking "potential long-term relationship." I made the first contact, emailing to apologize for how abrupt I'd been and explaining how I had left my notes in my dressing room. But even after exchanging witty, even flirty emails, I knew nothing about her.

Then fate threw me another billion-to-one curveball. Some Friday nights, I went to the movies with a woman on our staff that was strictly a friend. On that fateful Friday, my friend and I had loosely planned to meet at the theaters on 34th Street for a 5 p.m. movie. But when I called to confirm that afternoon, she didn't pick up and didn't call me back. To this day, I have no idea what happened to her. Maybe she had a better offer.

Now for the trillion-to-one shot: I had an answering machine at *Cold Pizza*, but I hadn't checked it for at least six months. Suddenly having unexpected time on my hands, I checked it. Ernestine had just left me a message, basically saying, "Hey, why don't we quit emailing and try talking on the phone?"

I immediately called her. She immediately answered. And we talked for two straight hours. Not one word was about sports. Especially on Friday nights, after I've done five straight two-and-a-half-hour shows of extreme sports debate, I'm happy NOT to talk sports.

Plus, it was clear from the start Ernestine knew next to nothing about sports, which I did NOT consider a deal-breaker. We could've talked for four hours—or six or eight—about movies and TV shows and music. We found we both love Woody Allen movies. She crazy-loves *I Love Lucy*. I couldn't match that, but *Lucy* was always my favorite childhood sitcom. Even though she's more than 10 years younger than me, I was surprised to find her favorite music is '60s rock and roll. Mine too!

This was meant to be.

Yet when I called my mother in Oklahoma City to tell her I was going out on a date with a woman from New York City whose mother was Jewish and whose father was Italian, my mother's reaction was, "Really?"

Really.

Football season was just starting when we met. Yet not only did she NOT balk at my watching sports at her apartment, she immediately ordered the TV sports packages required for me to watch my favorite college teams: the Oklahoma Sooners (I grew up in Oklahoma) and the Vanderbilt Commodores (I graduated from Vanderbilt). We found we also love the same food—low-fat, low-calorie, healthy cuisine. More and more we ordered in—a great advantage of living in New York.

One crucial aspect of our relationship is this: We rarely double date or go out to dinner with another couple (unless we are seeing special friends or it's for business relationships). We prefer to spend our Friday and Saturday nights together, just the two of us, usually at home . . . even if I have to watch SOME sports. When we're out with another couple, she and I can't talk to each other—not about anything that matters. Mostly, I end up talking sports with the guy, and Ernestine winds up talking whatever with the woman. I don't listen.

The point is that we don't need another couple around to help talk us through the evening. I am so thankful for that. That's the essence of our relationship.

Elsewhere in this book, Ernestine talks about my obsession with golf, which is true. What she doesn't tell you is that the moment I realized how much I loved her and wanted to be with her forever was on the golf course! So this is MY special golf story:

From the start of our relationship, Ernestine shocked me by volunteering to ride in the cart with me when I play golf. On vacation in Palm Springs, it will often be just the two of us because I like to pretty much have the course to myself by teeing off around noon with the temperature around 110. We load up the cart with ice and water, and she often drives while I play. I've tried to get her to play, but the closest she has come is playing putting games with me on the practice green.

I truly don't care if she plays golf, accompanies me while I play, or has anything to do with my golf. I have never applied the smallest amount of pressure. This is her choice. (But just between us, I really do like it when she rides with me.)

But this was the true man/woman test: Every July, I go home to Oklahoma City to play five days of golf with some of my childhood buddies. This has been an annual rite of summer for 44 straight years. The first year Ernestine went with me, I asked my friends if they would mind if she rode with me. This risked breaking the "man" rule: a woman invading our boys' day out? I promised she had learned golf etiquette and would not talk while they were in their backswing or about to putt, and would pretty much speak only when spoken to by them. I'm not sure they loved the idea, but after the first day, they were obviously cool with Ernestine riding along. Often, she just answers emails or texts, mainly for work, and sometimes she talks quietly on the phone if I park the cart away from the green. Sometimes she's only vaguely aware of what's going on with our golf. But if one of my friends strikes up a conversation with her, she comes alive. She has a personality that can win over the toughest doubter. My friends all love her now.

But think about Ernestine's initial dilemma: She could have spent the days in Oklahoma City shopping with the wife of my best friend, Craig Humphreys. Bev has become a close friend of Ernestine's. But Ernestine once again decided that I spend so much time on my job, and the two of us on a golf course is another way of being together.

Even if it meant being in a golf cart for four hours in 100-degree July heat.

But here's our occasional disconnect: I'm extremely competitive. Her, not so much. She has never been able to understand why I can get so mad playing a silly game. I can go as psycho playing golf as I can rooting for a game I've picked on TV. I just can't help myself.

Sometimes my friends and I barely keep score and just enjoy each other's company. But sometimes we play teams, more for pride than money. That's when it can get dangerous for Ernestine.

You see, I want her to show a little sympathy when I hit a bad shot. She's more likely to get mad at me for getting mad, which just makes me madder.

I often wish she'd just encourage me by saying, "You know you can play this game. I've seen you. Just relax and slow down and you'll get hot again."

I also think my friends play a little better when Ernestine rides along. Guys always want to show off for a female. That, too, can work against me: My friends are rising to the occasion, beating my brains out, while I'm getting madder and madder at her for getting mad at me.

But the incident in question had absolutely nothing to do with team competition or a spat with Ernestine. I was playing very well on my favorite course in the world, the East Course at Lincoln Park. On

No. 14, I crushed my drive right down the middle, leaving me only a short iron uphill to the green. I struck it perfectly, right at the flag, and figured I'd have a short birdie putt when we got up to the green. But I was stunned to find my shot had flown all the way into the back bunker. Now I faced an impossible shot out of the sand downhill to the pin. And of course, it rolled through the green into the bunker below the green. After I blasted weakly out of that one, my birdie was looking like a double bogey.

I was more frustrated than mad. Ernestine decided to "show support" by getting out of the golf cart and standing on the hill above the green to cheer me on. I flipped my sand wedge up to her before I putted, so she could put it back in my bag. I DID NOT THROW IT AT HER. But I shouldn't have even risked flipping it to her. It hit maybe three feet to her right, handle first, and caromed straight toward her bare leg. The blade of the sand wedge caught her right in the shin and opened a cut.

She was horrified. I was horrified. My friends were horrified.

We wet a towel with cold water and managed to mostly stop the bleeding.

Now came the big decision. The next hole, No. 15, is my favorite hole in the world: a downhill, dogleg-left par five reachable in two shots. I've birdied it many times and eagled it twice. I get to play it only one time a year.

I said, "If you want me to take you back to the car now, I will."

She knew how much No. 15 meant to me. She said, "No, I'm fine." She rode with her leg propped upright against the inner side of the door, ice wrapped around her leg in a Masters towel we borrowed from my friend.

And she toughed it out for the final four holes.

Not only that, but when we got back to the clubhouse, we re-examined the wound and decided it didn't look that bad. I wanted to practice my putting for a few minutes before we left. So she sat in the sun watching me—for maybe 30 more minutes.

It was at that point I decided I wanted to be with Ernestine the rest of my life. That was clutch toughness. That was sacrifice. That was loyalty.

In hindsight, we probably should have gotten a few stitches in Ernestine's wound, but instead, she proudly shows off her "golf scar" to all. And she definitely won ultimate respect from my childhood friends. I think they were thinking, "So that's why a guy from Oklahoma City is with a New York girl."

The New York girl changed my life. Because she didn't like sports, she actually started saving me from myself. Without her, I'd be watching sports even more—even games I didn't need for my show. Ernestine encouraged me to go to more theater in New York and to more concerts in LA. With Ernestine, I now take more long walks, during which we rarely if ever talk about sports. We always try to go to one or two movies a week and watch at least one at home on Friday or Saturday night (unless I have a crucial game to watch).

Ernestine and I will do just about anything to spend time with each other.

These are the ways we have carved out a life together, and given my crazy sports schedule, I don't have much life to carve. This is why she's so special.

Our relationship is far from perfect. We clash. We battle. I can get too intense and overemotional. That works on my TV show, but can be tough on her. And on us. Yet she often proudly declares, "They said we would never last, and we're still together."

Thanks to her.

Chapter 3

Ernestine Q&A

Why do women love guys who love sports?

There is a mystique around guys who love sports. It is fascinating to see a fully grown man hide his eyes during a play or turn off the TV, thinking the game will change if it is off and expecting his team to be winning when he turns it back on.

There is also a vulnerable, childlike side to men who watch sports. They get so excited knowing that their team is playing. They have their favorite spots to sit in, their favorite beverages and munchies, and their good luck charms, all while wearing their lucky sports jersey. It reminds me of kids on Christmas Day, running to open their presents: the same enthusiasm, joy, and sometimes disappointment! Is there anything more heartbreaking than a child not receiving that longed-for toy? Likewise, when a guy's team loses, it's a bad day.

How can you put up with watching all these games?

Since the first day I met Skip, I knew sports was a major part of his life and that if I wanted to see him on the weekends (or even during the week on certain nights), I would have to accept sports as my "friend."

The first few times I watched a game with Skip, I literally knew NOTHING about what was going on in the game. I knew there was a ball and that the objective was to score a touchdown, a three-point shot, or a home run. Beyond that? Clueless. And in those days, I didn't have the interest or the passion necessary to learn more.

But I DID have an interest in learning more about Skip. I knew that I really liked this guy, and I was determined to sit through this painful and endless parade of games, one after another, if it meant I was next to him. After a while, it became the new normal. Players' names began to stick in my head, and I began to remember the rules. That's not to say I studied or put in extra effort to learn—it just started to sink in naturally as I watched and asked questions. After all, I figured that if I was sitting there, I might as well TRY to understand what was going on.

Do you ever really get into the games, or are you pretending?

I never pretend to be into a game—you can't fake that. But after 13 years, I can honestly say that there are select games and teams I don't mind watching and, dare I say it, even enjoy!

After watching a team play for what seems like forever, I like to find out about their personal lives. It drives Skip up the wall, especially when it is a crucial moment in the game and he is hanging onto every play, and I ask, "Is he married? Does he have kids? Where does he live?" I just like to know about the people I am hanging out with for three, four, or five hours! Since I have no loyalty to one team over another, I usually ask Skip before the game starts which team he wants to win, and that decides my team. I am now a shirt- and cap-wearing fan of the San Antonio Spurs, Dallas Cowboys, and New England Patriots!

Did you always date guys who were into sports?

Until I met Skip, I had never dated a sports guy before. My "type" (a word we use before we meet someone who changes our life and is NOT the type we thought we were only attracted to) was always the artsy, long-haired, a-little-off-the-beaten-path kind of guy. When I started dating Skip, I told myself this would never last since he didn't fit the perfect image of my dream man in my head. But look at us now! Thirteen years into it and going strong! The moral of the story is to be open to all types because you never know who will steal your heart!

How do you manage your guy's jinxes?

This has been a learning process, and I STILL make a sports jinx faux pas now and then surrounding Skip's games. First, realize that everyone has a jinx of some sort. Maybe you don't think of them as real jinxes, and you call them something else: superstitions, feelings, whatever. If you think hard, you will find yours. For me, I will never walk under a ladder, I cross the street if I see a black cat, and I never tell a bad dream before breakfast (my mom told me it would come true otherwise).

I saw plenty of similar traditions in my own family growing up. My mom was a card player: if one of the guys in her poker game got up from the table to stretch his legs, she would say her game was over and she was going to lose—and then she would lose! My dad, being Sicilian, believed people would give him *il malocchio*, or "the evil eye." That belief is the reason you see people wearing "the horn," which they believe combats the evil eye. So after reflecting on all of my own nutty family jinxes, I have come to respect Skip and those millions of sports guys who hold near and dear to their heart their individual jinxes. It doesn't mean I believe in them or agree with them—I just give it up and let them be!

Do you adapt your schedule to what game is on?

Absolutely! I adapt not only my schedule, but also OUR schedule according to what game is on. I started doing myself a favor and began asking Skip a few days in advance, "What games do you have to watch over the weekend? Which are important, which are minor, and are there any you could miss?" That way, I could make my weekend plans without him, and I was less frustrated and disappointed. I found that it was much easier than making plans and canceling. When you know the game calendar and your personal calendar, you can plan to see movies, attend theater and concerts, and see friends without placing the cancel call.

At this point in our relationship, Skip is very good about telling me his "must watches," sometimes two weeks in advance. And if there is a special event I see we would want to attend, even a month in advance, he will go online and scope out the day/night game schedule before we lock it in. It is a give-and-take thing: he knows that I am sensitive to his schedule, so he will give it up to me on the days he has off and say it's my call. It's called balancing your relationship as well as keeping your own identity and life!

How do you find quality time with your guy when there are so many games?

Every couple has a different rhythm and schedule. Quality time does not always have to be hours at a time. Some of our best times have been during a 20-minute halftime. As the old saying goes, it's quality, not quantity! That statement holds true more than ever before when it comes to sports and guys. For 10 years, Skip lived five days out of the week in Connecticut while working at ESPN, and I lived in New York City. We shared a day and a half each week together in person, but we made the most of that day and a half, even with sports taking up some of that weekend. We called each other numerous times throughout each day, texted and emailed regularly, and hid notes and letters in the apartment for the other to find.

Do you and Skip have an agreement on how much away time you need together?

Again, my schedule living with Skip is magnified by one thousand, compared to the average sports couple, but we have dedicated weeks we know are ours. The week after the Super Bowl, we escape on a vacation where sports does not enter his mind or mine. We disappear again in June after the NBA season comes to an end, and we take a few more days in August, preseason NFL games, in which stars rarely or barely play. We fill those days with movies, theater, day trips, going to our favorite restaurants, and catching up with friends we rarely see. We may not do anything special, but not having to watch sports is special enough!

Have you started to enjoy sports more since being married to Skip?

I definitely enjoy it more, considering that I did not have any connection to sports before meeting Skip, so the smallest enjoyment is a big deal!

Have you started to understand the minds of men more since becoming a sports enthusiast?

Before, I thought it was just a game and guys watched it, the way we watch any show on TV. But the more time I have spent with Skip, I see it in a different light. There is a deeper connection men have to sports, which then carries over to their non-sports life. I believe it's a gladiator mentality: Men are allowed to yell, scream, shout, jump, and even cry together with other guys, even strangers, in one place while watching other men basically beat each other up in an arena—and it's legal to do so. It is a release that their everyday job does not allow. Most guys can't walk into their office and start ranting if they don't agree with their boss or coworker; they have to keep it in check (except for Skip, who gets away with shouting on air, but only sports-related shouting). Through sports, every guy in the world can blow off steam, not only for their game, but for their life.

Also, guys' personalities are revealed when you witness them watching a game. It is a great barometer on how they handle things in their non-sports life. Do they take their games seriously, or do they have a carefree attitude? If they lose, do they pout, or is it OK and he can go on his merry way without having a meltdown? If they are extremely competitive in sports, and he feels his team has to defeat his best friend's team, chances are he will be of the exact same mindset in other life situations not involving sports and games.

What are some ways you have found to keep interested in the game when your mind wanders?

Honestly, my mind wanders a lot while watching sports. That's when my Cute Guy/Cool Guy Tip kicks in big time (I will explain in depth in Chapter 5). I also try my best to appreciate what the guys are doing out there. When you break the game down, the fact is that every player wants to win. There is something about striving to be the best that touches each one of us, and we can relate to it. For that reason alone, I am fascinated by the stamina and willfulness you see exhibited on the screen, and you feel more invested in the game on a human level.

Chapter 4

Skip Q&A

In this chapter, I thought I'd pass the ball over to Skip to answer some of the most common questions I come across when talking with other women who are at their wits' end with their men.

Why do guys love sports so much?

I'm not sure my wife Ernestine will ever completely understand my obsession with watching sports. For now, I at least have an excuse: Watching sports 365 days a year is how I must prepare to do my job, which is a daily, live, unscripted sports debate for two and a half hours on FS1's *Undisputed*. But the truth is, I'd be watching sports like crazy no matter what I did for a living—maybe even more if I hated my job.

Obviously, watching sports is a guy's great escape. Ernestine watches Hallmark movies and endless house-hunting shows on HGTV. I watch the greatest reality shows on TV—wildly unscripted games with routinely shocking outcomes and superhuman performances under apocalyptic pressure, often featuring soap-opera backstories that make *The Young and the Restless* or *General Hospital* seem ho-hum. Almost every night, I am amazed by something I see while watching a game and can't wait to debate the how and why of it on tomorrow's *Undisputed*, when I hope many people can't wait to hear what me and my debate partner—Pro Football Hall of Famer Shannon Sharpe—have to say about THAT. Controversial calls by referees, tantrums thrown by superstars, and Twitter-rocking throws, catches, buzzer-beaters, dunks, or sound bites . . . every night, every Saturday, every Sunday. It's something you just can't imagine.

That something can consistently take you away from your real-world problems for a few hours. That something can be especially addictive to guys. No doubt females can get equally hooked, but not nearly as many as males, and rarely as obsessively.

Why is that? It often starts with athletic frustration. Girls obviously can suffer it too. But boys (unfortunately) can dream bigger in more sports. Boys can believe (at least for a while) that they're going to play on the biggest stages—in the Super Bowl, NBA Finals, World Series, Stanley Cup, or maybe even the World Cup, or individually in the Wimbledon final or in the final pairing on Masters Sunday.

Most boys try at least one of these sports at an organized level—and maybe three or four. Many are good enough to play on their high school teams. But the vast majority experience that moment of truth in which the realization hits you like a 250-pound linebacker or a 95 mph fastball: your sports career will end short of your childhood dream.

I grew up thinking I was going to play big-league baseball. My moment of truth came one cold day during spring break of my junior year in high school. This was in Oklahoma City, and I was the catcher for the Northwest Knights. On the mound for us that day at Southeast High School was Oklahoma's player of the year in basketball: six-foot,

10-inch Steve Mitchell, who had signed with Kansas State. As a baseball pitcher, he threw 95 mph.

Stepping into the batter's box to face Steve Mitchell in the bottom of the first inning was Darrell Porter, who the following year would be the fourth overall pick in the baseball draft to the Milwaukee Brewers. Porter would go on to start the All-Star Game as catcher for the Kansas City Royals and win MVP of the World Series for my favorite team, the St. Louis Cardinals.

That day, Steve Mitchell threw a 95 mph fastball a little high and inside to Darrell Porter, who batted left-handed. I reached to catch it, but it never made it to my mitt. That crack of the bat on the ball still echoes through my subconscious. It went off like a Fourth of July cherry bomb not two feet from my right ear. I'd never heard anything like it.

The ball rose . . . and rose . . . up into the gray gloom. A tennis-court fence maybe 50 feet high loomed in distant right field but never came into play. Darrell Porter's blast cleared that fence.

I heard the on-deck batter maybe 30 feet away mutter in awe: "No one's ever done that."

And I knew: I would never be able to do THAT. I would never be anything more than a pretty good high school baseball player.

Still, I'd been good enough to watch Major League games and occasionally wonder "What if?" What if I'd had a father or big brother who pushed me harder? What if I'd worked harder on baseball instead of spending so much time playing basketball (my first love, though I was only five feet, 11 inches tall) and golf (the most frustrating and addicting game on Earth)? Maybe . . .

The point is, I play baseball, basketball, football, and even golf at a high enough level to RELATE to the great players I watch. I have a pretty good idea what it takes. So do millions of other guys who had some early success in sports.

I love movies. But I often can't relate to, say, superhero movies (except for maybe *Batman*, though I can't relate to being billionaire Bruce Wayne). Movies are fantasy escape. Sports are reality escape. Sports movies? I've never been the biggest fan of them. To me, they often come off as corny, silly, far-fetched, or manipulatively maudlin. The actors often are rarely convincing as athletes, and the scriptwriters often just don't get it. Give me the real thing, live. That will always be unbelievably believable.

And, of course, give me a rooting interest. Lots of guys bet on games: sometimes with their hearts, sometimes with their heads. Many more play fantasy sports, which will force them to root for players on teams playing against their favorite team.

But we all have favorite teams, which brings me to a guy's deepest compulsion for watching sports: bragging rights. Bottom line, many guys watch sports so they can brag to their friends or coworkers about how THEIR team won. It's as if we're better men because we pledged allegiance to a team that just won the Super Bowl or college football's national championship. Sometimes, our very self-image can be attached to the outcome of our team's season.

Take me with my beloved Dallas Cowboys: My uncle took me to my first Cowboy game when I was 10. These days, I bet my public pride on them, game after game. If they win, I can open *Undisputed* by pounding the debate desk and yelling, "HOW 'BOUT THEM COWBOYS!" If they lose—especially if they really stink it up—I get ridiculed for two and a half hours on national TV. I'm sure many Cowboys fans can relate to my humiliation when they go to work the next day, especially if they work around fans of other teams, or around some of the millions who simply hate the Cowboys.

I guess you could go so far as to say I feel like less of a man if the Cowboys lose. Which is why I insist on watching Cowboys games strictly by myself. I cannot and will not inflict my bragging-rights torment on Ernestine. By myself, I can scream whatever words I choose to scream without having to worry about whether she's offended or scared or ready to leave me. I can scream at my coach or my stars or at players who SHOULD BE CUT TOMORROW.

On *Undisputed*, it's perfectly OK for me to call for the firing of my coach or the demotion of a player. But don't let Shannon Sharpe do it. Them's fightin' words.

I am also capable of going psycho during games played by my beloved Oklahoma Sooners. I can't help myself: it's in my blood. I was born into the Boomer Sooner tradition. My grandfather took me to my first game when I was five years old. On family vacations at ages six, seven, and eight—to Colorado, St. Louis, and New Orleans—I noticed that whenever we told people we were from Oklahoma, they inevitably said, "Oh, Sooners!" A college football team helped put my state on the national map. The dominance of our college football team helped erase some of the pain caused by the image beating my state took from John Steinbeck's *Grapes of Wrath*—about Okies who packed up and left the Dust Bowl in search of California's promised land. Oklahoma's self-image has long been attached to the fortunes of its Oklahoma Sooners . . . and now to its Oklahoma City Thunder.

Which brings me to a word I hate to use: hate. I suppose I don't HATE the University of Oklahoma's archrival, Texas, but I grew up strongly disliking everything about the Longhorns, from their Texas-sized arrogance to their team's color, that urpy burnt orange. Texas fans have long looked down on Oklahoma when they should have looked up to us. Our state is on top of their state! And starting in the 1970s, we Okies took great pleasure in the fact that we recruited teams that were made up 80 or 90 percent of players from Texas, and we went down to the Cotton Bowl each October and kicked some burnt-orange butt with our Texas defectors.

As a lifelong St. Louis Cardinals fan, I've always hated the Cubs. I can't help myself. It started in 1969 when Cubs third baseman Ron Santo started running and jumping and clicking his heels after Cub wins—a celebration that slowly faded away during the Cubs' historic September collapse. I hated Santo but later came to love him after I got to know him when I was the sports columnist for the Chicago Tribune. You see, Santo as a Cub turned my stomach and threatened my bragging rights in the hallways between classes during high school. It didn't matter whether or not he was the nicest guy on Earth, which he just might have been in real life. To me, from a distance, he was just the gloating leader of the archrival Cubs.

Same goes for the Eagles. Of the three Cowboy division rivals, I've always respected the New York Giants, and I've feared and loathed the archrival Washington Redskins, but I have always despised the Philadelphia Eagles. I don't like their seasick green uniforms. I don't like their fans, a bunch of Rocky Balboas who booed and threw snowballs at Santa Claus. I don't like how full of themselves the Eagles get when they beat the Cowboys (which hasn't been that often). We always put the Eagles back in their place, which has often been last.

I know: this is all completely irrational.

But all this is why I can't stop watching sports . . . and why my wife will never quite understand.

What do you feel is a fair amount of game time vs. family time on weekends?

I believe Ernestine will attest that I try hard to make time for us on Friday nights and Saturdays—even on college football Saturdays.

Friday nights are always date night. I'm off the air by 9 a.m., so we usually go to a movie on Friday afternoon, then watch our taped episodes of *Jeopardy* and maybe another movie on Friday night. Occasionally, I'll have a must-watch NBA game or World Series game on Friday night, but I'll pick my spots. I'll watch the score on my computer or phone while we watch two or three episodes of *Jeopardy* or maybe the first half of a movie. Then maybe I'll pick up the NBA game at halftime or even wait until the fourth quarter, or maybe I'll wait until the fifth or sixth inning of the World Series game. Then she will gladly watch the rest of whichever game for the next hour or so. Then we get back to "date night." It's not perfect, but it barely works.

On college football Saturdays, it's possible I have important games from noon Eastern time until 1 or even 2 a.m., so I try to rank my games in importance. We go to lunch when I feel I can afford to miss the first half of the next game. I will watch the score on my phone, then hope I can get away with just watching the second half.

But when NFL playoff games are scheduled on Saturday, I'm sorry, but I'm out. And every NFL Sunday, I'm out from 1 p.m. Eastern until midnight.

This is the best I can do. But I don't play poker with the guys on Wednesday nights or golf on Saturdays or Sundays. Every waking second I can devote to our relationship, I do. In this game, I believe I can play for a tie, which is better than the loss of my marriage.

Does it bother you that Ernestine doesn't know anything about sports?

When we got married, I knew Ernestine didn't know or care about sports. I talk and think about sports so much that I need some breaks. With Ernestine, I'd much rather talk about movies or books or pop culture or just life. Constantly talking about sports with her would be way too much of a good thing—apple pie and ice cream all day and all night. You risk losing your taste for it.

I've never asked Ernestine to watch a game with me. But I don't mind if she does, especially if she appears to have some genuine interest. She has come to like pro basketball. Not college, just the NBA. As opposed to helmeted football players, she can see the faces of pro basketball players . . . along with, of course, their physiques. She particularly has fallen for my favorite team, the San Antonio Spurs. Some nights when the Spurs are on and I'm trying to watch while prepping for my show, she'll choose to watch the Spurs by herself in the living room. She'll even come running to my door to say "Did you see that shot?" or "That was not a foul!"

Pretty cool.

But the important point is this: I've never demanded or so much as even asked her to watch a game with me. It's her choice. But I do enjoy her company during games when she's really into them.

Can I really jinx my husband's team?

The real question here is "Do you really believe something that happens in your house in Los Angeles can negatively impact the team you've picked to win a game being played in Dallas, San Antonio, or Norman, Oklahoma?" The answer is the bane of Ernestine's existence: YES, I DO.

I realize this is insanely preposterous. But I've demonstrated to Ernestine again and again how jinxes constantly haunt me during games if not carefully avoided.

Here are my jinx rules: I tell her if she's going to watch an important game with me, she cannot come and go or she'll risk changing the momentum. I've proven to her again and again what happens when I turn on a game halfway through, and the momentum immediately and dramatically swings the other way. Run-of-the-mill games, fine, she can catch a few minutes here and there if she chooses. But big games, she must commit to staying—or to not watching at all.

But I must admit, I have asked her to join me if my team is getting annihilated in hopes she'll change my luck or their biorhythms. I must admit I have awakened Hazel, our two-year-old Maltese, from a deep sleep in her doggy bed to bring her in to watch a game with me because my team is playing like dog doo-doo and I hope Hazel's presence will change that. And yes, even when Ernestine has committed to watching an entire game with me, I have asked her if she wouldn't mind leaving the room for a while if my team is inexplicably choking its brains out and I am losing my mind.

I know: inexplicably insane.

If she's not watching a game I'm winning and at halftime I happen to walk past her on the way to the kitchen or bathroom, she knows there is one thing SHE CANNOT SAY. She cannot say, "You've won this one." Kiss of death. Invariably, my team will fall apart and blow it.

During this year's AFC Championship Game, she broke (or, more accurately, shattered) another simple jinx rule by knocking on my door to ask a question that easily could have waited until after the game or even until Monday. No exaggeration: the moment she stuck her head into my office, where I was watching alone, Tom Brady made the worst mistake I've ever seen him make in a playoff game. The Patriots (my preseason pick to get to and win the Super Bowl) were no more than a half-yard away from Kansas City's end zone when Brady failed to see Chiefs linebacker Reggie Ragland and threw it right to him for an interception. NOOOOOOOOOOOO!

But it happened, just as she opened the door. I tried to yell, "No, don't!" but I couldn't stop her. And Brady committed a shockingly uncharacteristic cardinal sin. See?

Yes, I sometimes lose touch with reality while watching the best reality shows on TV—my games. But this is just the way it is and always will be. Forgive me, Ernestine.

What faux pas do women make when talking about sports that embarrass men?

Sometimes we'll be with friends and Ernestine will try to relate an anecdote about watching a game with me—usually a jinx incident. Her play-by-play jargon will be so wrong or misleading—as if she's speaking Greek about a play that happened in Japanese—that I will have to take over so the guys at the table aren't completely lost when she gets to the punch line. I just reset the table and let her deliver the punch line. I don't condemn her; I actually applaud her for trying. She just doesn't know, and I don't care.

The other mistake many women have made in my presence is to give a backward score. If you say, "The Cowboys won 16 to 24," you're disqualified as a sports fan. It's like saying, "I had a jelly and peanut butter sandwich." It's just wrong. The winning score always goes first. The Cowboys won, 24–16.

I want to start liking sports so I can hang out with my guy. How do I start to care if I don't?

The best place to start is following the soap operas of sports. It will be next to impossible to quickly learn and become conversant in game strategy or player strengths and weaknesses. But guys are just as interested in the soap operas—which we talk about on *Undisputed* as much or more than we do what happened in games.

Start reading the sports websites and getting a feel for the issues affecting your guy's favorite teams or the best teams. For instance, Bill Belichick wanted to cut or trade Tom Brady before the 2018 season and move forward with his man Jimmy Garoppolo, but the owner, Robert Kraft, overruled Belichick. LeBron left his home area of Cleveland (he's from nearby Akron) for Hollywood and the Lakers, but at least he had returned to Cleveland after "taking his talents to South Beach" to play for the Miami Heat and helped Cleveland win a championship in 2016. Cowboys owner Jerry Jones has almost always hired weak yes-men coaches (like current coach Jason Garrett) who are happy to serve as his puppets. Kevin Durant left Russell Westbrook in Oklahoma City because he was tired of Westbrook shooting too much and wanted to win rings with Golden State (he has two and counting). Kyrie Irving got sick of LeBron being a drama king and forced a trade to Boston, where he has occasionally struggled to lead his own team.

As long as you gain a basic understanding of the subplots, it will be much easier to grasp the in-game developments. You might even find yourself turning into—dare I say—a bona fide sports fan. Who knows? Maybe one day your guy will complain that YOU want to watch too much sports.

Chapter 5

The Cute Guy/
Cool Guy Factor

adies, you know there has to be a deeper reason for sitting through HOURS of game after game after game.

For me, the best part of any game is finding a cute guy or two on each team and making them your own . . . in other words, make it worth your time. This is the same way our guys watch some of the shows WE love—not for the storyline, but for the Hot Chick Factor. Turnabout is fair play. In football, the tight ends *do* have tight ends. The reason I like basketball more than football is that basketball players wear only shorts and tank tops. No helmets and shoulder pads and long pants. Watching basketball, you can actually see muscled-up shoulders and biceps and pecs and quads and calves.

Soon after I was introduced to the world of sports, I realized I had to find a way to stomach all of these games. Since watching was not in my DNA, I thought long and hard about how I could achieve this. After working in fashion for many years, one of my responsibilities (and, I must admit, fun perks) was to conduct model go-sees. That's where a company calls in 10 to 20 male models in hopes of finding one that will work for an upcoming catalog shoot or commercial. I took the same approach with athletes. With so many players on one team, my mission was to find one or two I considered the best looking or most interesting and make them my reason for watching.

Basketball, football, baseball, golf: so many men, so many choices. Go-sees had nothing on my new fun hobby: combing through a roster of athletes was like being stranded on a fantasy island occupied solely by men.

Hey, if guys can go to Hooters or strip clubs, we can at least admire the physiques and hair and faces of athletes either overclothed (football, baseball, hockey, golf) or somewhat clothed (basketball). Of course, I'm looking strictly from the perspective of a woman attracted to men. But this obviously can work in different ways for all genders in relationships with sports-obsessed partners, husbands or wives.

For sure, THIS can work regardless of sexual persuasion. My Cute Guy Factor often turns into a deeper bond—the Cool Guy Factor. After the initial attraction, you start to get to know somebody you're forced to spend so much time with, and you develop a deeper appreciation and connection. Skip has his favorite players based more on their performance—how exciting they are to watch or how clutch they are in late-game, do-or-die situations. I have my favorites based on their backstories, their away-from-the-game lives, and their nonsports stories. Some guys caught my eye, then my heart. As the old saying goes, "Beauty is only skin deep."

I researched their backgrounds as if I were hiring them for a job. Not the way guys do when they choose their fantasy teams, when stats are everything. I needed personal info. I needed to know their dating history, if they had a famous girlfriend or were married with kids.

Skip has been a San Antonio Spurs fan since the 1980s, and his love for the Spurs has infected me. Now I love them almost as much as he does. He appreciates that they play basketball "the right way." Meanwhile, I appreciate their great bodies and good looks. In 2013, my selected Cute Guys were Tony Parker, the baby-faced point guard once married to Eva Longoria; Tim Duncan, the strong, silent type at around seven feet tall; and Manu Ginobili, the tall, dark, and handsome Argentine with the sexy Euro flair.

Connecting with players led to a deeper engagement with the team and fandom. I've even bought Spurs sweatshirts with my guys' numbers on them. I've worn them proudly up and down Eighth Avenue in NYC, and I love it when I pass somebody who yells their traditional battle cry, "Go, Spurs, go!" While I usually sashayed around the Big Apple in my Gucci's and Manolo's, I'd fallen for a team from "the Alamo City" nicknamed for the jingly-jangly things cowboys hook to their boots to spur their horses.

I started ranking Cute Guy/Cool Guys the first year I dated Skip, and I've had a new batch every season since. It actually has become an exciting game to play because there are always trades, free-agent moves, and rookies. Discovering a new team member to add to the mix is what keeps this game alive and never boring. Sometimes, I even find myself sitting on the couch before Skip does just to watch my men play.

Here are a few of my favorite players—and least favorites:

LeBron James—I'm torn about him, but I'm more pro than con. I like his devotion to kids. I don't like this new Hollywood mogul thing he has going on. Skip pretty much likes LeBron personally, but isn't a fan of LeBron as a player—Skip doesn't think he has the "clutch gene" late in close games. I don't care about that. I still have LeBron on my "good guy" list. I wouldn't give him First Team All-Handsome, but he's entertaining to watch. He always has entertaining soap operas swirling around him, so I'm often quietly rooting for him while Skip is rooting like crazy against him.

Lonzo Ball—I feel bad for him: his dad LaVar has overshadowed his career and life. I think he is a nice kid who needs to break away from his father.

Rajon Rondo—I have a special place in my athlete world for Rondo. I loved him as a Celtic . . . not so much as a Laker. I do think as he got older, he has become more affected and arrogant, but I'm still keeping him on my favorite list. I feel like I grew up with him as an NBA player. He was by far the youngest on the championship Celtics, but it was always like he ran the show for Paul Pierce, Kevin Garnett, and Ray Allen. He just always played with such quiet confidence for such a little guy.

Kyle Kuzma—Such a super nice guy in interviews. So respectful. So cool. So talented. Plays so hard every single second.

Steph Curry—Sorry, not a fan. I really hate watching him play with his mouthguard hanging out of his mouth and all of his hot-dog, show-off celebrating. Skip loved him when he was at Davidson and pushed for him to be drafted first overall ahead of Blake Griffin. But Steph has become really egotistical over the years, and for me, too big for his britches.

Kevin Durant—I have a love/hate relationship with Kevin. He trashed Skip a few times when he was playing for the Thunder—in Skip's hometown of Oklahoma City. And I cannot let go of that. I have softened a bit towards him now that he's a Warrior, but I will not forget the nasty things he said about Skip.

Draymond Green—No love lost. After he called LeBron the "B word," I lost respect. Always complaining to the refs. Always taking shots at opponents in interviews. Just completely unlovable.

Klay Thompson—I really like him. Classy, great shooter, and always gives a great post-game interview with humility and sportsmanship.

Andre Iguodala—Nicknamed Skip "The Diabolical Hater" years ago, and it has always stayed with me. I try to like him, but . . .

Gordon Hayward—Love his look: he's handsome and could have a second career as a model. As much *GQ* as NBA . . . plus his game lives up to his looks.

Al Horford—One of my favorite guys. I've been watching him so long I feel like I know him. It's like he's part of our family. Despite being an older guy, his energy and spirit outshine a lot of the younger players.

Kawhi Leonard—One of my all-time favorite players, and this is one guy where Skip and I definitely part ways. Skip believes he "quit" on the Spurs last season just to force his way out of San Antonio. So Skip won't even say his name anymore—he just refers to him as "No. 2." I like him no matter where he goes, Toronto now or one of the LA teams next year. Sorry, Skip. I've always loved Kawhi because he has always been so "Kawhi-et"—sorry, quiet. Because he never said much, there was always a mystery around him. His hairstyles are always so cool. And he just plays with this badass toughness. He's my guy, Skip.

Marc Gasol—I loved watching Marc play when he was on the Grizzlies. He was SO BIG, but so nice. I think he and his brother Pau are the coolest brothers in the NBA, and it has always been fun watching them play against each other. They grew up in a family of doctors, they're very family-oriented, and they're two of the nicest guys in the NBA, so respected by players and coaches.

Danny Green—Loved him as a Spur, and I still love watching him play as a Raptor. My connection? He and I come from the same town on Long Island, so I have a special bond with him.

James Harden—He can "shoot the lights out" with his three-point shots. His beard drives me crazy and I want to cut it shorter. But he just keeps making spectacular shots. Nonstop scorer. Always entertaining.

Chris Paul—If I see one more of his State Farm commercials, I will scream. 24 hours a day. For a while, they were all about him and his twin brother, Cliff Paul. Now it's about his insurance agent who somehow seems to live with him. That's all I can think about when

I'm watching Chris Paul play—his twin brother and his insurance agent. Just ruins it for me.

Ricky Rubio—My secret crush. Love his long hair he wears in a "man bun," and he has piercing eyes with that Euro style. Great flair as a player. My favorite.

Kyle Korver—Another great-looking guy. Has bounced around the league but has hung on because he's such a great three-point shooter. He's old school, he's spiritual, he's a family man, and he works with underprivileged children. My kind of guy.

Dirk—No last name needed. One of the first NBA games I watched with Skip was Dallas Mavericks vs. Phoenix Suns. Dirk caught my eye immediately at seven feet tall. Looked like a warrior in a medieval romance novel: long, wavy, sandy-blond hair, strong nose, chiseled face. He's an unbelievable shooter and scorer for such a tall man. I have loved him ever since. Sorry to say he just retired. Sad to think I'll be watching the Mavericks without him.

Dwyane Wade—Another superstar who just retired, only D-Wade was even beyond Dirk for me. D-Wade WAS basketball. Great player, great personality, great dad. Winner. It just won't be the same without him—even though he twice beat the team Skip and I love (the Spurs) in the Finals.

Tony Parker—He's still hanging on with Charlotte after a long, great run with the Spurs. Another of my all-time favorites. Tony has charm, coolness, and a super sense of humor. In his prime, nobody was quicker than Tony Parker. He was just a blur to the basket. The Spurs miss his big-shot making.

Tim Duncan—The Spurs have always been my team (because they were Skip's team when I met him), and Tim was the greatest Spur. Just such a nice guy. So quiet, so classy. No showing off or gloating or trash talking. He just played—played the way few ever have.

Manu Ginobili—I proudly wear a Manu sweatshirt. He defines class. Family man, beloved by teammates, and respected by every rival. OK, he was maybe the greatest flopper ever, exaggerating contact to draw fouls. But he just played with such style and flair and constant motion and energy. A great Manu memory was when he captured a live bat with his bare hands that had flown into the arena during a Spurs game. Now that's a tough guy.

Patty Mills—I adore Patty, with his Aussie accent and funky hair. Not even six feet tall, but he is always such a spark plug. He's the spirit of the Spurs—almost like a mascot on the bench or court.

Russell Westbrook—Pushes the envelope with his fashion style, but he has attitude and is secure in what he wears. Coolness on and off the court. But he often plays so angrily that he makes himself hard to love, unless you're a Thunder fan.

Kevin Love—Not only is he a great player and a great interviewee—so smart and open—but the bonus for me is he is the nephew of Mike Love, a lead singer of one of my all time favorite bands, The Beach Boys.

Dak Prescott—He is a "friend in my head" because Skip has always liked him and I've been watching him since he was at Mississippi State. I like the little bow ties he wears at the postgame press conferences—he's kind of "nerdy cool." He always plays with guts and strength. I love the way he leads the Cowboys.

Ezekiel Elliott—Too many tabloid headlines for me. He's just been involved in too many scandalous situations to be able to believe him. He obviously was suspended for domestic abuse. I think I grudgingly accept him because Skip loves him as a running back and Skip loves the Cowboys so much.

Jerry Jones—Another guy who's just hard for me to trust. Always smiling. Ever the showman. Just seems like he wants to be the biggest star on the team. But because he owns and operates Skip's Cowboys, I bite my lip and tolerate him.

Aaron Rodgers—Next to Chris Paul, he's in the most TV commercials—"Discount Double Check," more State Farm—which just wears me OUT. Always seems to be dating starlets. Now he's with Danica. I just wish that on the field, he could live up to all the hype.

Tom Brady—He's been part of my family for the last 15 years. His family is our family. I "live" with him. He won me over early because he was man enough to wear (and advertise) Ugg Boots, which are often seen as women's footwear. He's a Renaissance man. He can wear his hair long or short. He doesn't have to act like a typical macho football player. Yet he's the greatest football player EVER. I love that.

Baker Mayfield—Skip grew up in Oklahoma City going to University of Oklahoma football games, so he was on fire with Baker as soon as he transferred to OU from Texas Tech. I now know his life story. He's egotistical, but he's Johnny Manziel without all the career-threatening off-field issues. He's so fun to watch. Plays with such swagger and emotion. Always puts on a show.

Cam Newton—A favorite of mine because of his great style. An extraordinary collection of hats, casual outfits, and suits that he wears in his postgame interviews. An absolute unique style and flair. Like Tom Brady and Russell Westbrook, he just doesn't care what anyone thinks of him. Always entertaining, on and off the field.

Pete Carroll—I've had a crush on him since I first started watching college football in 2005 and he coached USC. He was like a permanent kid who treated his college players like friends. Even now, at age 67, coaching the NFL's Seahawks, he still has his boyish charm, forever a frat boy, always chewing gum on the sideline. Always upbeat and excited, and that becomes contagious for his players. Still looks like he surfs, or like he could be a lifeguard. He's my guy.

Richard Sherman—He's the only NFL player I despise. He's arrogant, rude, and classless. He once attacked Skip for no reason during an appearance on Skip's old show *First Take*. To me, he has problems. But Skip always says he has been a very good cornerback.

Antonio Brown—I know him as much from *Dancing with the Stars* as I do from football. He has charisma, a great smile, and a fun personality. Willing to try anything in the dance competition. I know he's been involved in lots of Steelers controversy. Maybe he got a little too carried away with himself. But I still like him . . . no matter what Skip has said about him on *Undisputed*.

Larry Fitzgerald—The classiest player in sports. So involved in helping kids. His dad was a sportswriter like Skip was. Intriguing, unique style with his long braids, he is one of the greatest receivers ever. Wish they all could be like Larry Fitz.

TIPS

PICKING YOUR OWN CUTE GUYS/COOL GUYS

Start out with your guy's favorite team(s) (applicable to any sport), force yourself to sit through one game, and take notes regarding which players jump off the screen at you. It's not all about looks: charisma, attitude, style, and toughness comes into play when choosing your own CGCG. Jot down their jersey numbers and names, and don't forget the team. While in the process, you will also be watching his opposing team: start on their players list as well. Soon you will find you have CGCG players on almost every team in that league!

Once you start your list, Google the players and read their Wikipedia pages. You will be surprised to find interesting backgrounds, family information, and fun facts that make up each player. Trust me, the next time you watch a game, you will remember your CGCG's off-court life the minute you see them. It will create a bond between you and your new CGCG, as well as a better connection between you and your partner.

Chapter 6

What to Say or Not Say When His Team Loses

I will start off by saying that even if his team loses and he acts like it is the end of the world, he will survive. I have lived to see this and tell! The phrase "This too shall pass" pretty much sums it up.

Over the years, I have discovered you're never going to win when his team loses. There are no right words OR wrong words to say when his team loses, or worse, gets blown out and embarrassed. No matter what comes out of your mouth, it will end up like a dagger in his heart. What I do know is that you need to be delicate when you approach the subject.

My first year dating Skip, I had no idea what to expect after a loss. This was so new to me and, honestly, I had never had to deal with this before, so I was in the dark.

In my mind, I equated his losing a game to my missing an episode of

one of my favorite shows like *House Hunters International*: there always seemed to be "another game" almost every night of the week (NFL and NBA schedules were not a part of my life or mind)!

Of course, I thought I was being sympathetic by saying "Sorry about your game. Don't worry; there's always next time!" To Skip, this was me showing no compassion. The longer I dated him, the more I realized this was going to be a bigger challenge than I could imagine.

"Next time" does not count in a guy's life when it comes to losing. It is monumental. Sulking, pouting, and grimacing are common facial expressions after a loss. What worked for me was to offer up my condolences and then leave him to work it out of his head and heart on

his own. This is a moment when he needs time alone to reflect on what exactly happened during that play or what strategy could've changed the outcome. He will beat himself up until exhaustion sets in emotionally and physically. There are times when Skip says he needs to "talk it out" and go over what he thinks took place, so I listen. In reality, he just needs an ear, and sometimes, you have to be that ear!

But as sure as the sun will come up tomorrow, you will see your guy coming back to life in a day or so. He will begin to eat again, chuckle here and there—and before you know it, like a wilting daisy in need of rain, he will spring back to life just in time for his next game!

TIPS

WHAT TO SAY OR NOT SAY
WHEN HIS TEAM LOSES

Everyone needs "their space" after a disappointment, including when his favorite team loses, so give your partner some space AND a break! As my mom would say to me when my Italian dad was not in the best mood for whatever reason (most likely it involved one of his workshop tools breaking when he needed it the most), he needs time to "cool off" . . . so let him be alone and chill. It will do good for both of you, and once he regroups, you can resume your normal life.

Guys really feel their teams are part of the family, so you need to treat their loss seriously. I know that sounds pretty wacky, but the best thing you can do is say "Sorry for your loss!" Crazy, right? But believe me, he will accept it and feel as though you really get him, and he will appreciate your concern.

Chapter 7

What's Up with His "Team's Logo on Everything" Collection?

I live with a man who has a long history—almost a love/hate relationship—with the Dallas Cowboys. His closet is filled with items emblazoned with the team's star: T-shirts, baseball caps, player jerseys, socks, pens, floor mats, and even a Sharper Image floating Cowboy helmet halogen lamp I gifted him for Christmas! And that's not to mention all the merchandise bearing the emblem of the San Antonio Spurs, Skip's other favorite team.

I must come clean and say I have contributed to both teams' merchandise sales by purchasing my own Cowboys and Spurs shirts and caps. Of course, the No. 1 reason is to support my guy's teams, BUT I will confess that I do like the team colors, and some of my best "cute guys" play for them.

I have been fascinated all my life by watching guys sport so proudly their teams' T-shirts paraphernalia. I knew there had to be some deeper, psychological meaning for this obsession. So I dug a bit deeper . . .

This merchandise has a dual purpose. First, for your sports enthusiast, seeing another person wearing his team emblem on a shirt fosters an instant connection. This shared identity might facilitate communication among individuals or just increase a feeling among fans that they have shared values. For many, their team colors are a representation of their hometown: the streets they grew up on and the people they lived among. A shirt represents more than a team: it represents a community.

Second, they can serve as good luck charms! There are lucky jerseys, hats, sneakers, T-shirts, socks . . . the list goes on and on of what sports fans will wear to help their team win, or in some case won't wear if they fail to come through. Wearing a hat facing forward? Turn it backward and maybe the team will score. If that happens, you'll never wear that hat with the brim facing forward again during a game. Unless . . . it causes fumbles and interceptions for the opposing team.

TIPS

LOGOS ON EVERYTHING

There is a very simple solution that will benefit both you and your partner when it comes to his countless team logo items: create a space solely for his priceless things. By divvying up a specific area for all of his team stuff, he will feel that you understand his sports needs as well as respect his sports love.

Every once in a while, buy him a new logo addition for to his collection. It can be as little as a keychain or cup holder. It will make him smile and know that you are rooting for him and his team.

Chapter 8

The Sports Calendar

So this is me: When I'm not working, I am pretty low-key. I like spending time at home with Skip and Hazel, I love watching my always-happy-ending Hallmark movies, and I enjoy catching up with my gal pals both in NYC and LA. I'm not someone who needs people around me all the time; I'm actually a bit of a loner. Skip and I truly enjoy each other's company; most of the time, we love just hanging out together.

That being said, there are times when we look forward to seeing friends and partaking in nonsport-related activities.

After the first few months of dating Skip, I began to see a pattern in his life that I knew would eventually be mine, and it hit me like a brick.

If I intended to stay in this relationship, anytime we wanted to do something fun in the real world (outside of his games), I would have to plan it around his never-ending sports calendar. I soon found out I was not alone. Some women even plan their upcoming weddings around their husbands' college football games. Yikes!

Skip and I both love movies, especially matinees. Squeezing them into his Saturday schedule during NFL or NBA season has become as complicated as me understanding football rules.

I remember one Saturday in particular: Skip said the noon games weren't all that important to him, but he absolutely HAD to be back for the start of a 3:30 p.m. life-or-death matchup. The movie we wanted to see would supposedly end at 3:20 p.m., depending on how long the previews went. So I agreed to either leave the theater early or miss the end if the movie ran past 3:20 p.m. If it ended on time, we would need to make a literal run for it on Eighth Avenue, weaving in and out of wall-to-wall people—not easy to do.

As you could imagine, the pressure and stress were off the charts. My imagination and built-in craziness kicked in: "What if we can't get back to our apartment because the fire alarm has gone off and the elevators are shut down? What if I twist my ankle while we're running? What if our cable has gone out and we don't know until he tries to turn on the game?"

Bottom line, the movie ended at exactly 3:25 p.m., and we both ran our butts off down Eighth Avenue and made it back to the apartment just as the game was kicking off at 3:32 p.m. Saved!

Buying any type of ticket in advance, especially for the theater, is a risk. I learned that lesson after throwing away 300 dollars on Broadway tickets simply because the team he didn't care about two months prior (when I purchased the tickets) had gotten crazy hot and now was THE TEAM playing THE GAME of the night, which started exactly the same time as our show.

Thanks to the never-ending game schedule that rules our lives every month (except some of July), our vacations are squeezed in around varying dates of Super Bowls, NBA playoffs, and so on and on and on. Over the years, I have become wiser and more mature on how to deal with this craziness in a calm and compromising manner.

TIPS

LIVING WITH A SPORTS CALENDAR

Ask your guy for a two- or three-month layout of his games. That way, you can project good weekends vs. bad weekends for the two of you.

Plan a fun "girls shopping afternoon" or "chick-flick movie night" when you know he has a special game to watch. He will be happy to know you are enjoying your time with friends, and you don't have to hear the moans and groans in the house.

Find his rare low-sports weekend and accomplish the one thing you have been talking about doing together for a long time! Take a drive, hit Vegas for a weekend, or book a five-star hotel near your home and escape for a sexy getaway.

Chapter 9

Women at Games

Ladies, it's time for a hard truth: Either show a little interest or don't show up at all.

I chuckle when I'm watching a game on TV and the camera pans across the stands and catches numerous women who look like they're going clubbing rather than sitting at a Dallas Cowboys game. Wearing sky-high heels, evening lingerie, glitzy makeup, and hair—but even more ridiculous than their game attire is the "I don't want to be here" look. You know the ones: they're texting or otherwise engrossed in conversation on their cell phone, clearly not discussing the latest touchdown. Not only are they embarrassing themselves, but their guy as well.

When you commit to attend a game, do your best to be there—not just physically, but mentally and emotionally.

Imagine if the roles were reversed: You invite your guy to an event—maybe a birthday party, dance performance, wine tasting, etc.—and the entire time you're there, he's on his phone with his friends or watching a game on his tablet. How would you feel? Would you question his support for your interests? Would you apologize to your friends for his behavior? Basically, all you need to do is follow the golden rule and treat your man the way you want to be treated.

TIPS

LOOKING THE PART WHILE WATCHING THE GAME

As the saying goes, "When in Rome . . ."

Why not invest in a few pieces of "game clothes": apparel and footwear that is versatile enough for wearing to any sports event. As a reminder, I have never played golf in my life. I occasionally putt with Skip, drive the golf cart, and really enjoy the peace and tranquility the open course provides. But at the same time, I look the part of a golfer. I had a ton of fun buying cute skirts, cardigans, and an assortment of visors, hats, and accessories for all those special golf-day outings.

Prior to meeting Skip, I really had no clue what to wear on a golf course, but I quickly realized that my Lululemon leggings and James Perse T-shirts would not cut it. So now you have the green light to shop till you drop, and discover a whole new look you never imagined would exist in your wardrobe.

Chapter 10

How to Survive the Holiday Sports Room

Family get-togethers can be stressful enough given different personalities, past family grudges, politics, and disappointing food. But then we add salt to the wounds by creating the dreadful "game room," otherwise known as the living room or TV room.

This is where all the nice, sweet uncles, brothers, cousins, dads, and brothers-in-law gather to watch the game (or games) of the day and turn into the Hulk!

It is also where the shouting, cursing, yelling, and parting of the family ways take place. My one and only suggestion is this: STAY AWAY FROM THIS ROOM.

When it comes to guys and their teams, male pride takes over, and even the most loving son and dad all but enter the UFC Octagon.

I have tried to sit in for a few minutes to see what was really going on, and within seconds, my stress level rivals the noise level. Everyone is yelling and screaming not only at the TV but also seemingly at each other.

Remove yourself from this hysteria and hide anywhere else in the house. Trying to blend in or become a part of that room just won't work. It's what I like to call THE SPORTS TWILIGHT ZONE. Once you step foot inside, you may not come out the same person . . . or ever come out at all.

But don't worry: all the drama and craziness will fade, usually in time for leftovers. Sure, some of the guys will keep the trash talk going the rest of the night. But remember that it has to stop at some point. There are more games tomorrow, and the next day and night.

TIPS

SURVIVING THE HOLIDAY SPORTS ROOM

Best plan of attack is to be one step ahead of the game . . . literally! Make sure you take a look at the TV guide a day in advance and note what time the games begin. That way, no surprises when the room empties out and there's an immediate vacancy around the table.

For those not partaking in watching the game, schedule a fun group walk in the neighborhood or chat time with relatives you have not seen for ages. Plan outside activities away from the mayhem and head back once you know the games are over.

Not sure you know when the games are over while walking or chatting? Keep checking the sports websites like ESPN.com. They provide minute-by-minute updates on all games being played, as well as let you know when halftime rolls around. And more importantly, when the game is over, find out which team won so you can be prepared before heading back to the game room with a thumbs up or "sorry for your loss" face.

Chapter 11

Golf

---

*G*olf is a sport that takes four to five hours to play. Skip lives to play golf.

Even on his worst golf day, when I hear for the 100th time how he shouldn't be allowed back on the golf course, I know two days later my phone will ring and he will tell me he is on his way back to the course to hit balls at the driving range, or to practice his putting and maybe even to play nine holes (which usually turns into 18). Because his time is limited, Skip doesn't mind playing by himself, or occasionally with just one buddy. Rarely in foursomes or fivesomes. But sometimes—get this—he likes when I join him! Crazy, right???

Make no mistake: I am not a golfer. I have never played, except if you count miniature golf, and sometimes putting with Skip when he is done playing 18 holes.

He tells me he likes my company. I think it's because he has no pressure since I am not critiquing his every shot like golf partners do. The biggest hoot is that I actually don't mind going with him. I put on my cutest golf attire, pack my iPad, make sure we have plenty of water and ice in the bucket, and turn the golf cart into my office for the day.

There are a lot of guys who play golf just to get away from their wives or girlfriends. Most think their partner would hate being out on the range. That's not us. Golf is an escape, but never from each other.

The truth is, there's something about it I like. Courses are serene with beautiful landscaping. The mesmerizing soundtrack of birds chirping . . . the freshly-cut grass that looks and smells SO GREEN . . . the whole nine holes—I mean, yards. For me, golf is zen and tranquility.

If you live in a big city, a golf course is almost like entering a sanctuary. The world stops. I can spread out, think, write, do nothing at all except just BE! My mind is as free as a bird. If I choose to work, I can—I just have to pick my spots and keep it down if I talk on the phone. Texting and emailing are the best ways to do business while literally smelling the flowers and seeing the occasional fox, squirrel, deer, or (yuck!) snake.

It's also a chance to break from my fashion routine. Being a true New Yorker, my wardrobe is generally a sea of black, but for some reason, being on a golf course makes me want to wear color! I have an extensive wardrobe of cute short golf skirts, polo shirts, and cardigan sweaters in fun pinks, greens, yellows, and paisleys! It helps me get into the spirit of the moment and disconnect from the outside world, even if I am writing a PR pitch.

I know this is hard to believe, but now, incredibly, I don't mind watching golf on TV with Skip. Over the years, I've had my favorite golfers: Fred Couples, Sergio García, and Bernhard Langer (who kind of looks like Skip). All of this amazes me because I still have no desire to PLAY golf.

TIPS

GOLF ETIQUETTE AND RULES

Talking loudly on a golf course is a no-no, so keep your conversations low. This is a place folks need to concentrate on their next shot, so soft and low is key!

If your guy (or anyone else in your group) is just about to take a swing, please don't ask them a question or offer advice. It totally breaks their concentration and can wreck their swing.

If you're at a country club or on a private golf course, cell phones are a complete no-no. Before you freak out, take a deep breath. It's all OK. It's time to give your ear and brain a break for a few hours. It'll do you some good!

And here comes another jinx rule: NEVER say, after he hits a good drive, long down the middle of the fairway, "You've got this hole." Kiss of death. The golf gods can get angry. The demons can get a hold of your guy's psyche. A birdie can turn into a triple bogey. A ball can bounce inexplicably into a sand trap. A putt that's right on the line can suddenly detour to the right or left for no apparent reason. And you've jinxed him again!

Chapter 12

Breaking into a Multigenerational Sports Family

When I met Skip's family and spent time in Oklahoma City, things crystallized for me regarding how this sports fanatic came to be. The Bayless family was University of Oklahoma and Dallas Cowboy fans all the way. His grandparents and parents were invested in these teams, as were all of his friends. Imagine this: he had just started kindergarten and he was already an old pro, going to games. Sports was not something he and his family did just to pass the time: it was part of their history and a community cornerstone.

Just to recap, I did not come from a sports family. My brother and father liked soccer, and sure, Dad watched the occasional baseball game, but they weren't crazy fans. We were not the type of family that bonded over games and tailgated together. My family went to museums, art shows, and classical concerts. Even though we lived two hours outside of New York City, and both my parents grew up in NYC, we simply had no sports history in our genes.

So when Skip first told me about the Sooners, it honestly took months for me to figure out what the heck he was talking about! (Yep, foreign language again!) His entire family and all of his hometown friends worshiped these teams, wore the garb, and went to the games. I couldn't have been more of an outsider. He explained that when he was growing up, Oklahoma City had no teams other than minor-league baseball and hockey. Now, of course, OKC has the NBA's Thunder. But in his childhood, Skip had only his Cardinals up in St. Louis and his Cowboys down in Dallas. That meant his University of Oklahoma Sooners became his city and state's "pro" team.

This happens, of course, in many regions of the country. But few college football programs have had as much historical success as Skip's Sooners. He told me that he first realized the magnitude of this phenomenon when he and his family took a vacation to, say, New Orleans. When people asked where they were from and his mom or dad said, "Oklahoma," the inevitable response was, "Ahhh, the Sooners!"

Skip said his state took such an image beating from John Steinbeck's book *The Grapes of Wrath* and the subsequent movie starring Henry Fonda that the OU football team actually helped restore the state's national reputation. As much as I've tried, I still can't quite grasp the depth of this. It's like Oklahomans somehow think they're better people when kids recruited from Texas and California and Florida carry OU to the national playoffs. I think they're pretty cool people with or without OU football. But I'm from New York, where college football was never that big a deal. I mean, we always had the Yankees, Giants, Jets, and Mets.

When it finally came time to meet Skip's family, we flew out to Oklahoma City, he bought me an OU hat in the airport gift shop, and I jumped right into it.

The culture shock was immediate. Teams, players, and coaches were included in the dinner conversation as if they were relatives—quirky, sometimes disappointing relatives, but beloved nonetheless. At first, it seemed so weird and foreign, but the more I was around it, the more I came to respect it. In the Bayless home, as I am sure it is in homes all over the country, the love of sports creates a special closeness and connection. No matter what problems or issues the family faces, their love for their teams remains a connecting thread for all. When Skip wears an OU hat or shirt, it isn't just a representation of his team; it's a reminder of his grandfather who took him to his first game when he was five years old—ironically and painfully, OU's first loss after what still stands as the longest winning streak in college football history, 57 games, ended by 18-point underdog Notre Dame. Skip still talks about what a long silent ride home from the stadium it was as after that game. He could still use some therapy to deal with that memory.

I think I have done a pretty good job of becoming a part of Skip's OU world. I've tried to learn all I can about the histories of OU and the Dallas Cowboys. I sport their baseball caps, T-shirts, and sweatshirts, and I can hold my own in team conversations when we go back to visit Oklahoma. I think I've done enough to at least earn honorary membership.

TIPS

BREAKING INTO A MULTIGENERATIONAL SPORTS FAMILY

Once you discover their team, take a few minutes and Google the history. It will help you understand the team's backstory, key players, and current news surrounding them. You will not only be able to understand the dinner table conversation, but you can also partake in it.

Buy yourself an official team's baseball cap and T-shirt. It's the least you can do to show your guy you are supportive of his team. His family will be impressed as well.

Ask your guy his earliest family sports memories. I guarantee you will see a different side of him: a softer and nostalgic side he may not always display.

Chapter 13

How to Keep Your Love Alive When You're on Opposing Teams

As you know, over the years I have acquired my "cute guy/cool guy" list, which is players on teams I find attractive and edgy that make the game more bearable for me to watch. They have become my "friends in my head," and I have a loyalty to them. No matter where they go, what team they are traded to, I still want them to win.

And this is where the home trouble begins!

As much as Skip loves the Cowboys, Spurs, and Sooners—and Tom Brady, though not really the Patriots—Skip picks games from day to day on his show with his head and not his heart. As much as he wants the Cowboys to win another Super Bowl, he doesn't believe they're going to go 16–0. He'll occasionally pick, say, the Eagles to beat the Cowboys in Philadelphia. His debate partner Shannon Sharpe might say,

"The Cowboys are going to KILL the Redskins by four touchdowns," after Skip has picked the Cowboys to win a close game. Then Skip will respond, "OK, give me the Redskins plus 25 for a case of Diet Dew." They're always betting cases of Diet Mountain Dew, Skip's favorite soft drink.

I can't keep up with all of his night-to-night rooting interests. I just like my "cute guys" and my favorite players, even after they're traded. I fell head over high heels for Paul Pierce, Ray Allen, and Rajon Rondo when they won their championship with the Celtics. And I couldn't help rooting for them when they wound up elsewhere. This nearly ended our relationship the night of Game 6 of the 2015 NBA Finals, when the San Antonio Spurs were visiting the Miami Heat. Skip, then on ESPN's *First Take*, was at the game, but he and I kept talking by phone during timeouts.

Obviously, Skip was rooting for his beloved Spurs, AND he had picked them to upset the Heat of LeBron James and Dwyane Wade ... and former Celtic Ray Allen, "my guy."

The Spurs were up three games to two and looked like they were in control late in Game 6. Finish it off, and they would have been the first team to win four games in the best-of-seven series, meaning they would claim the NBA championship. I could hear in Skip's voice that he was tasting it. The Spurs were up five points with 23 seconds left, then three points with seven seconds left when LeBron missed a three-point attempt. For a split second, it seemed like the Spurs had won ... but Chris Bosh moved quickly to grab the long rebound. He passed it into the corner to Ray Allen, who then made what Skip always calls "the greatest clutch shot in NBA history."

I was like, "YESSSS—oh, no."

I was so happy for Ray ... and so upset for Skip.

Ray's three-pointer tied the score. The Spurs lost in overtime, then lost Game 7 and lost the Finals.

And for one night, I was in danger of losing my relationship.

After a few quiet days, Skip finally said, "Look, I like Ray too. Good guy. One of the greatest shooters ever. But he shot me right in the heart."

I'm sorry, but I still love Ray and ask Skip from time to time if he thinks retired Ray could still play. "No," Skip always says. "But I'm sure he can still shoot."

Now, when Skip is rooting against LeBron's Los Angeles Lakers, I try to keep a lid on my emotions when it comes to LeBron's teammate, Rondo. Skip never did like Rondo. But if I'm waiting for the start of a Laker game, I often wave at the TV and say, "Hey, Rondo, remember me? I'm still here rooting for you."

Skip just rolls his eyes.

TIPS

KEEPING THE LOVE ALIVE WHEN YOU ARE ON OPPOSING TEAMS

If there was a lie-detector test set up in my home asking to whom the players matter more, me or Skip, I think you know the answer. In the end, when I root for my player over his, it's really for fun and sometimes, between you and me, just to "get his goat." But if I see his team losing, and the tension is building, I dial down my ribbing. Call me a softie, but I feel bad for him since his stake is much bigger than mine in the game.

Word of advice: know when to let it go. Best to smile and console than to jab and laugh at him. Remember, long after the game is over, you're planning on cuddling up with your real partner that evening, not your TV player!

Chapter 14

The Sports Swear Jar

*I*think we can all relate to this. Even if you think you live with the most mild-mannered guy in the world, that all changes when **HIS GAME IS ON!**

All of a sudden, you witness a transformation reminiscent of Dr. Jekyll and Mr. Hyde. Who is this guy? What did you do with my husband? My sweet, lovable man is now ranting and raving and cursing like a lunatic!

I hate to say it, but you're not going to be able to stop this. Sports and guys swearing are like bees to honey: a natural combination.

However, there is something you can do to moderate this, but only if he is willing to play along. If so, then you have a good chance of not only tapering off the steady stream of profanity, but also walking away with the goods!

Create a swear jar: each time he curses, you get the reward. Instead of dollar bills, I prefer "wins." For example, you choose the next movie, he cooks dinner for you, you get to pick the restaurant on date night, he buys you that handbag or dress you've had your eye on, or you get your choice of massage: foot, back, and head!

If he can actually last one full game without swearing, he then reaps the reward: breakfast in bed, a back massage, an extra two hours of sleep, etc. To spice it up, add some sexy coupons to the mix. There are plenty to choose from, so use your imagination.

TIPS

CREATING A SPORTS SWEAR JAR

At the start of each new sports season, sit down with your partner and unveil this fun and rewarding program.

Ask your guy to write down on a piece of paper his 10 "fantasy wins." They could be as simple as watching Monday Night Football completely uninterrupted, or as intimate as full-body massages three Friday nights out of the month. Then you do the same. The sky's the limit! Cut them up and place them in an empty shoe box with a lid. Bring the box out and place it in the TV room at the start of the game, and let the SSJ fun begin!

Chapter 15

Fantasy Sports

Fortunately, I haven't had much first-hand experience with fantasy sports—Skip's already living most men's fantasy, so he doesn't really need another outlet.

Your guy might be another case, though. And, trust me, I get it: it probably looks really weird to an outside observer.

If you haven't been clued in by your guy, here's how fantasy sports work: At the beginning of a season, guys enter local or online fantasy leagues and draft their own fictional teams using real athletes. During the season, they calculate each of their players' individual, real-life statistics (points, touchdowns, home runs, etc.) to figure out whose fantasy team is winning. Basically, every guy acts as the manager of his personal dream team, and then they use a bunch of math to declare the winner.

If that sounds strange or out of character for your guy who hasn't done math since he graduated high school, I get it. But do you remember what Skip said back in his Q&A chapter about why men love sports? He talked a lot about how sports are an escape and how watching sports is a way for them to connect with something they dreamed of playing as kids.

Think of fantasy sports as a step further. Guys playing fantasy sports don't just want to watch the success—they want to be a part of it. Skip has no use for it because he doesn't want to root for random players on teams playing the team he picked or is rooting for: "Just too much of a conflict for me," he says. "I just don't need fantasy. I'm betting my pride on games, not to mention cases of Diet Dew, every day on national TV. But I understand why men and women want to prove to their friends they have superior sports knowledge by assembling championship teams. I've always thought I could be a good NFL or NBA general manager—in fact, I've had GMs tell me I could've been pretty good. But before every real NFL or NBA draft, I'm betting my pride that this quarterback will be better than that one and this two guard will be a better scorer than that one. So I'm playing my own version of fantasy, in reality. And if I'm wrong about a player, I'll look like a fool on national TV."

Many women play (and sometimes dominate) fantasy sports. I've learned a lot about sports, but maybe not that much. But for sure, just about every fan has a strong opinion about every big trade ever made, believing his or her GM is either a genius or the biggest idiot in sports history. Fantasy provides a fan with the opportunity to prove he or she is better than his or her GM. I love that. And for the fan who lives on batting averages, free-throw percentages, and other second-level statistics, it's a great way to live out the fantasy while spending time with friends. There are much worse ways your guy could spend his time away from you.

Chapter 16

No One Likes a Jinx

This happened fairly early in our relationship. I had just returned to our apartment at 54th and Eighth Avenue after picking up dinner—Chinese and our once-a-week Ray's Pizza. He was sitting in the dark watching an NBA playoff game featuring a frequent on-air target of his: LeBron James. Without thinking, I turned on the kitchen light, which sent some light into the living room where he was watching.

"Wait . . ." he said, and then paused to watch what I didn't know was the final play of the game. LeBron took an in-bound pass from a teammate and shot it from about three miles away from the basket. Skip groaned like I had kicked him in the groin.

LeBron, whom Skip often (and rightfully) criticized for not having "the clutch gene," had hit a rare, huge clutch shot to beat the Orlando

Magic and tie up the series, one game all. On air the next Monday, Skip would call it the "Shot Heard Round the World."

It was also the "Shot Heard Round My Apartment." Skip couldn't speak for the next three or so hours—another rarity—and when he finally cooled off, he said something truly shocking.

"You jinxed me," he said, shockingly matter-of-factly.

"I what?"

"When you turned on the light, you changed the game," he said.

"Wait a second . . . me flipping a light switch in New York City somehow changed the direction of some stupid basketball shot in Cleveland, Ohio? If I have that much power, I should go buy a Lottery ticket."

"You changed the game," he muttered, somewhere between devastated and furious.

"Maybe I should change boyfriends," I said, my father's Italian temper flashing in me as I stormed off to call my Jewish mother.

I had been called a lot of things in my life, but never a jinx. I'm a sucker for old movies. To me, a jinx was the bimbo ex-girlfriend who walks into the casino and jinxes the no-good gambler into losing all his dough. But my mother reminded me that she also believed in jinxes.

"What have I always said?" asked my mom, widowed and 78 at the time. "When I buy a lottery ticket and the guy behind the counter says, 'This one's a winner,' I throw it right in the trash. It's jinxed. And when I'm playing poker and one of the guys gets up to stretch and walks behind me, I always yell at him, 'Don't do that! You're jinxing me!'"

It was like the aftershock after the Manhattan earthquake: Even my dear mother believed in jinxes. I should have known: She grew up with Gypsies and fortune-tellers on the Lower East Side of Manhattan. She convinced me to try making peace with and comprehending the many and various forms of sports jinxing my husband bizarrely believed in.

Yet I did try to reason with him in a rare quiet moment between games, appealing to his spiritual side: "We go to church every Sunday. You believe in God, and you always tell me not to pray for your teams to win because God doesn't care who wins games. So how can you believe in some weird power of jinxes?"

"I can't explain it. But they're real."

For the record, Skip doesn't bet money on these games—he bets his national-TV pride, which I totally get. I feel for him when he gets ridiculed by debate partners in front of millions of viewers (in addition to Twitter, Facebook, and Instagram followers) who are gleefully aware of which team he picked to win. There are times I would like to punch the guys on his show who are teasing him about losing. I may not know a ton about sports, but I do know that I love him, and no one messes with my guy. He then has to remind me this is his job and he loves what he does, win or lose!

On one occasion, after a particularly heated disagreement about jinxes, I called my friend Francesca for advice. She called me back with her therapist on the line. I gave them the blow by blow of the situation, and then asked how to handle and remain in a relationship with a guy who is obsessed with and possessed by sports.

Her response was very matter of fact and concise: "Dear, there is no fix to this. There are a few cold-hard facts here. Men love sports. Men are not going to give up sports for their ladies, and if they do, they will be miserable. It's in their blood. Here are the remedies: You can leave him, or, if that's not where your head is at, I suggest you start taking notes and figure out his sports triggers. If you know turning on a light switch in his mind changes his game, then don't do it. If getting up to use the bathroom in the middle of a game is an issue, then don't do it. It's all a matter of learning the script. Unfortunately, I can't tell you what other things constitute a jinx in his head; that's the question you need to ask him. But before you take the plunge, maybe you should wait until this game is over tonight. For both your sakes."

You better believe I've taken that advice to heart. Over the years, I've developed a list of general rules to avoid jinxing Skip and his games, while also keeping my sanity.

Maybe your personal list will look similar to this:

1. Never, ever say the team he's rooting for has won before the game is over.

2. You cannot walk into the room in which he's watching an important game, sit down, and start watching with him mid-game. If you're going to watch with him, you must start from the beginning.

3. If he's rooting for a team that's losing badly, and you happen to walk by the living room, and he asks what you're doing, and then engages you in conversation . . . WATCH OUT. If, during that exchange, his team shows any sign of life, he will ask you to sit down. If good things keep happening for his team, you are stuck on the couch for the rest of the game. You have now become a good-luck charm, an antijinx, and you are stuck in that seat for the duration.

4. If he finds a "lucky spot" to stand or sit in during a game, you cannot ask him what in the name of the Long Island Medium he's doing. Above all, you cannot make fun of him—not without the risk of a knockdown, drag-out, "I-want-a-divorce" fight.

5. Moving or changing the decor or items in a room once a game starts—such as opening the blinds if they're closed, removing pillows from the couch, or, the mother of mistakes, turning the lights on or off—is a big no-no.

6. He believes in jinxing himself. Here's how: If we come back from eating dinner out, and he turns on a game that was just so-so, not that important, and if the team he picked is way ahead, once he turns the TV on, his team will start blowing the lead. He is convinced that this is real and he's jinxed himself by turning it on. There are times when he refuses to turn it on at all and will monitor online so that his team will win. He'll say to me, "Do you see what just happened? I JUST CHANGED THE GAME AGAIN!" I've seen this for myself, but I still believe it was just the players having an off night. To Skip, it was his jinx power.

As time has passed and our relationship has continued to grow, I've come to get a handle of his jinx thing. I'm not saying I accept, understand, or buy into it. In fact, I would like to go on the record by saying that I DO NOT BUY IT!

But, to keep peace in the Bayless household, I try to think one step ahead of him and his jinxes when we are watching games. Even if I'm not watching the game but I am in the same house, my antenna is up.

This is all very challenging. So allow me to share with you some more of my run-in jinx stories.

Never Call a Game

In June of 2013, our biggest jinx incident took place. This was the precursor to "my guy" Ray Allen shooting Skip's Spurs in the heart late in Game 6 of the NBA Finals.

Skip was in Miami. LeBron's Miami Heat vs. Skip's Spurs. The Spurs were up three games to two. Win this one, and the Spurs were NBA champs.

With 18 seconds left, the Spurs took a five-point lead and, in my euphoria, I called his cell phone. The second I heard his voice, I screamed, "WE WON!"

What I couldn't hear was him saying, "Don't say anything." But I did, and I said it LOUDLY.

He later told me, "You know how every once in a while you hear something and you suddenly get that sinking feeling because you just know in your bones what's coming? I just knew it, and it was not good."

Here we go: I was the reason the Spurs blew it. No matter what I said, making sense with an out-of-control sports guy was pointless. He was going to believe what he believed, no ifs, ands, or missed putts.

So now for some heavy-duty, play-by-play, basketball talk. This is how it went down:

The Spurs missed a free throw. Then they missed another free throw. Then LeBron hit a three-pointer. Then LeBron missed a three-pointer—he "LeBricked" it, Skip said—but the Heat got the rebound and passed it into the corner to Ray . . . who made what Skip still calls "the greatest clutch shot in NBA history." Tie game. Overtime.

The Spurs lost in overtime, then lost Game 7 in Miami and lost the NBA championship I prematurely proclaimed they'd won. It was my fault, because of something I said over a phone from Manhattan to Miami. Somehow, I had upset the universe, releasing cosmic shock waves that caused the Spurs' free throws to veer off line and fail to fall through the basket.

I kept trying to reason with him. I kept saying, "Do you realize how insane this is?"

And he said, "I realize how crazy it sounds. But trust me: you blew the Spurs' championship."

Lucky Spots

During the 2014 NFL season, out of the blue, Skip decided that he had found his "lucky spot" from which to watch Tom Brady's Patriots. Maybe my prayers were answered: He had picked the Patriots to beat the Seattle Seahawks in the Super Bowl.

Of course, he chose to watch the game from that season's "lucky spot," sitting on my side of the bed in the bedroom. I was in the living room, watching the game, while also watching a Turner Classic Movie, at the same time talking on the phone.

I didn't hear much coming from the bedroom for most of the evening. Every time I checked on the game, it just looked pretty obvious that Seattle was better. But as I flipped back and forth during the fourth quarter, I was surprised to see that Tom Brady was bringing them back. Then at the end, it just got crazy. I must admit, I didn't really get what had just happened.

Skip burst through the door with both arms raised and yelled, "Did you see that?!"

"Yes," I lied.

"The Patriots won!" he yelled, doing a little victory dance with his arms pumping toward the ceiling.

"I know," I lied. "Congratulations."

"Aren't you happy?" he asked incredulously.

"I'm happy," I said, still pretty lost about what had just happened and trying not to show it.

He sensed I didn't quite get it, so he explained: "Seattle had the ball at the Patriots' one-yard line at the end, so if they get just one yard, they score a touchdown and win. But, they decided to throw a pass instead of just handing the ball to Marshawn Lynch . . ."

Lynch, I knew. Beast Mode. He's the guy who wouldn't talk to the media all week before the Super Bowl, who just kept saying, "I'm just here [at the press conference] so I don't get fined." The only reason I knew that is because Skip would tell me about it every day after his show. I also remember because I found it amusing that the Beast Mode was the one who ate Skittles before and during every game. Now I was on solid ground.

He continued: ". . . and Russell Wilson threw it, and a rookie for the Patriots who didn't even start the game and wasn't even drafted—a rookie out of West Alabama!—A ROOKIE broke in front of the receiver and intercepted and SAVED THE GAME!"

Now he was losing me, but I pretended I understood. All I knew for sure was that he was VERY HAPPY and that he (and I) wouldn't have to dread doing his show the next morning. He had correctly predicted the game.

Once again, he was convinced his lucky spot had changed the game. He said, "I didn't say a word the whole game, even when it looked like there was no way. I just sat right there on your side of the bed and hung in. And it worked AGAIN."

No, it didn't. The rookie from Northwest Alabama Southern or whoever just did a better thing than Seattle did. That's all.

But as long as he was happy, I was happy.

You have to understand, there had been many lucky spots before this one. There was one season that his "lucky spot" turned out to be in the corner of the kitchen. So he would stand for hours in that corner watching the game. He would hop back to his spot like a bunny to place his glass back on the table before any bad vibes come through! He even ate his full dinner standing. *You* try making dinner, maneuvering around

him, and serving it up—it's not easy to do. After all, if he moves from that spot, the game is over, and guess who's to blame?

Another time, he was washing his golf clubs in the kitchen sink during a game, and as soon as he started, his Spurs began a historic play-off comeback against Steph Curry's Warriors. Needless to say, he continued to wash over and over and over again the same club faces until a player we both love, Manu Ginóbili, hit the game-winning three-point rainbow. A whole hour of washing and rinsing and washing and rinsing.

Now I'm brainwashed.

After that Super Bowl, Skip made it clear that his "magic spot" on my side of the bed would never work again. No "same time, next year."

What worked in 2014 would not work the following NFL season. Next year would be a whole new adventure for me.

A Different Kind of Jinx: The Stuffed Kind

About three years into our dating life, I bought a stuffed bear designed by Dennis Basso for QVC. Yep, I love QVC, and at times Skip has watched with amazement and even asked questions about the segment or hosts. Of course, he won't admit it publicly, but he laughs every time the cooking segments air with David Venable doing his happy dance. Skip cracks up!

So when the two-foot-tall little bear joined the household, Skip immediately said, "QVC?" Yep, he's made out of the same faux fur Basso's coats are made of.

The stuffed bear caught my eye, and I couldn't resist. I figured he would make a great mascot for the house since we didn't have a dog or cat at the time.

Skip thought I was out of my mind, but I didn't care. "Bear," as I named him, lived on our bed.

Soon after, while watching QVC once again, I discovered Basso also made a dog, a Scotty with red hair—and he was on sale! I thought Bear needed a friend, so "Dog" moved into the house and also onto the bed.

Skip thought I was even more insane but didn't say much except, "QVC?" Then he added, "Maybe you should think about getting a bird? Or maybe some fish?"

Nope. I thought Bear and Dog made great additions to the Bayless household. No mess, no barking, and when they chat, they keep their voices low so as not to disturb us.

So, what does this have to do with a jinx?

As they say, there is more than one way to skin a cat, and there is more than one way to ward off a jinx!

After about six months of Bear and Dog living with us, I noticed that during Skip's games, the stuffed duo was always sitting on the chair or the couch.

I thought maybe Skip brought them in to accompany me.

That is, until one day when I overheard Skip telling Bear and Dog that his team was winning, and it was all because they were sitting next to him.

I couldn't believe my ears.

Two stuffed animals changed my guy's game? Now I really was thrown for a loop. Not only am I dealing with a guy who thinks I'm a jinx if I walk into the room and sit down, but now my guy is using my innocent stuffed animals to save the night.

Thinking about how to approach this subject weighed on my head for days, but I didn't want my little guys being used as lucky Buddhas all in the name of sports.

So, of course, I asked Laura, my good friend and doctor, to weigh in. She laughed when I told her. "My husband has something similar! There's a small brass turtle he uses as a paperweight, and when he watches a game, he places the turtle on the seat next to him. All hell breaks loose if I move the turtle to sit down, and he'll say there are plenty of seats in the living room and 'Why must you move 'Timmy?'"

I felt a bit better. I'm sure there are thousands of men (or even women) with the same "disease," and we need to learn how to accept and treat it by opening our eyes and minds to an alternate universe: sports!

A Living, Breathing Jinx

In August of 2016, after four months of living in our new LA condo, I decided we needed a new family member.

We needed a puppy.

Just the way he's a sports guy and I'm not a sports girl, we both liked different dogs. What a surprise, right? Skip loves Rhodesian Ridgebacks and German Shepherds—you know, big, tough dogs. My dream pooch, however, was a teacup Maltipoo or Yorkie.

After I announced my pup was going to be the size of a grapefruit, Skip's exact words were "I will ignore it, I don't want to play with it, and I don't want to know it. He can be your dog."

I'd say, "How can you say such a thing? They're so adorable!" He would look at me and say, "I'm not stopping you from thinking that."

Since I was working from home instead of an outside office, I won out.

Enter Hazel Bayless. A she.

Hazel is a Maltese and named after one of my favorite TV shows from the '50s, starring actress Shirley Booth. She is feisty, aggressive, spunky—a total spitfire. She has also grown beyond the size of a teacup to somewhere in the soup-basin range . . . a good seven pounds of athletic muscle! My dream of keeping Hazel in my little handbag à la Paris Hilton went right out the window when she hit five pounds.

Along with the weight surprise came the biggest shocker ever: Skip is so in love with this dog, it is unbelievable. He treats her like she's an athlete, and she loves it, wrestling and playing chase with him. He's also thrilled she has grown beyond the average teacup size so he can take full advantage of her strength, quickness, and toughness. Hazel has become the daughter Skip never had, and he is so proud to prance her around and show her off. She's become the star of his Facebook Live chats, the darling of *Undisputed*, and a favorite of Skip's three million Twitter followers. She loves him back just as hard. (Reminder: This is the same man who declared he didn't want to be in the same room with "it" or tell anyone we owned a Maltese!)

But now we get into deeper waters.

One night after dinner, I went searching for the little princess, and she was nowhere to be found. I was frantic, thinking she had run out the front door and down the hall. But suddenly, I could hear laughing and barking coming from the back room.

Then I heard Skip say, "Way to go Hazel. Good girl."

I walked into the room and saw Hazel and Skip sprawled out on the couch.

Skip, always the truth teller and never a liar, looked like a deer in headlights. "Wait a minute," I said with a smirk. "You're not using Hazel as your good luck charm, are you?"

"No, never! It just so happened she was in the room with me when the Spurs started winning."

"You know what's going to happen," I said, half laughing. "One of these days, Hazel's good luck charm is going to turn and she will become the new jinx, and then what? I live it myself! Poor, poor Hazel."

A few days later, it was the same ritual: Hazel disappeared from sight as soon as the game was on. That is, until I heard Skip yelling, "Oh, no. Oh, no! Hazel, it's time for you to go back in the living room."

He carried Hazel out of his TV room, arms extended, holding her as if she had a run-in with a skunk, handed her to me, turned around, returned to his "man cave," and shut the door.

So every now and then Skip will invite Hazel to watch the game. As he does, I ask him how important the game is. He then rethinks it and goes in the back room alone, just the way she and I like it!

A Hotel Dilemma

When Skip and I finally decided to move to LA, we flew out to find a place to live before we made the BIG move. We stayed in a hotel for a few days just to scout out the neighborhoods. Usually, I make all the trip reservations, but this time Skip had a few thoughts he needed to share.

"Did you know that on the first night we arrive, there's a big NBA game that I have to watch?"

"Yep, I do. So what else is new?"

"And the second night, I have another game that I can't miss."

Why did I feel this was leading up to something?

"So what are you trying to tell me?"

"Well, I'm going to throw this out. It doesn't mean I don't love you, and after all, we're going to be together for the rest of the trip, so I was thinking . . ."

Before he could finish his sentence, I knew where we were heading. He wanted two rooms, and the word "jinx" was part of this equation.

Never in my life did I dream of going on a house-hunting trip with my fiancée and staying in two different hotel rooms. I mean, what were the hotel people going to think?

"What's the matter?" I asked. "Do you think I'm going to jinx you? Is that it?"

"Well, yes! You know what happens sometimes when we sit together. I can't risk any outside forces jeopardizing these games. They're too important to me. And I don't want to risk me getting mad at the game and you getting mad at me and us having a fight as the game is being won or lost. I apologize in advance, but I think it's best. Maybe we can ask for two adjoining rooms so we can be next to each other and visit."

If he wasn't so cute when he uttered those words, I would have hauled off and socked him with the pillow from the couch, but at this point, I was so over it all that I gave up. "Sure, sounds great. I'll ask for two *adjoining* rooms."

We arrived in LA, rushed like lunatics from the airport to the hotel, just so he could make it in time for the start of the game. We checked in, I gave up caring what the hotel people thought, and I settled into my room. I ordered room service for both of us and decided to chill and watch a chick flick on the pay channel. I heard his game through the door but drowned it out by turning up the volume.

I was very happy, and I didn't have to deal with play-by-play commentary. But no more than 10 minutes into the movie, I heard a knock on our adjoining door.

"Oh, no," I thought, "this can't be happening. Maybe they sent him the wrong food?"

I shouted through the door, "Hey, what's up?"

And then I saw the handle of the door turn slowly, and my nightmare was coming true. He was about to give me the play by play of the game even when I was in a separate hotel room!

"Do you have the game on?" he asked.

"No, I'm watching a movie."

"Turn on the game for a sec: you have to see this replay. Kevin Durant got away with an offensive foul. He charged!"

Hard to believe, but I actually knew what that meant! I guess 12 years of watching sports with Skip had rubbed off on me. He grabbed my remote and flipped to the game.

At this point, I saw the writing on the wall, and I said, "Do you want to sit in here with me?"

"No, I'll watch it in the other room, but what do you think? Do you think it was a charge?"

It all crystallized at that moment: "Ernestine," I thought, "this is the man you love, the man you're going to marry, the man you're moving cross-country with, and the man who has driven you up the wall with his sports thing since the first day you two met."

When I would complain to my mom about the sports thing, the jinx thing, and the game thing, she would say, "You need to ask yourself one question: Are you happier with him or without him?"

That conversation popped into my head immediately as Skip sat on the edge of my bed. I answered by saying, "I think it was a charge."

As he walked back into his room, I decided to keep the adjoining door open. I stayed in my room and, instead of the movie; I decided to watch the game.

So, Mom, I think you know my answer!

By the way, his Spurs won a playoff game that night at Oklahoma City. He was so happy.

How to Avoid Being Called a Jinx

- Refer back to Skip's jinxes in the beginning of this chapter. Your sports guy's jinxes may look different, but they'll prepare you to expect the strangest possibilities.

- Ask in advance how important the game is he's about to watch. There are some games that mean more than others. That way, you can gauge his mood in advance. If it's a so-so game, he may be a bit looser and not scrutinize everything you say or do, and the jinx thing may slide!

- Keep yourself busy if you choose to watch the entire game with him. I always have plenty of what I like to call my "rag magazines" next to me. You know, mindless fun reads like *People, Star, The Enquirer,* etc. That way, the time passes quickly and you can kill two birds with one "rag." Satisfy him and get your reading finished.

- If he asks you what you think a player should do before a certain play (if his team is winning and he's in a good mood), say you'd rather not say. Too many times I fell for that and innocently threw out my two cents. Holy cow, if it turns out the player does what you suggested and his team goes south, watch out. The blame will come back to you and your jinxing!

- Always ask in advance what games he needs to watch this week or weekend. That way, you can plan ahead and not spring on him at the last minute "Bob and Deb are meeting us for pizza tonight" just as he turns on the game and settles in for the duration. Better to know in advance so there are no surprises for either of you!

- Don't rearrange the furniture or the décor: A change in the home space could "result" in a loss. Also, don't do any major clothes washing that day; you could wash one of his "lucky" items (T-shirts, towels, socks, etc.) by mistake. All can wait until after the game.

Chapter 17

Celebrity Connections

Skip and I have a special connection with each of the celebrities that follow. They happily shared their personal thoughts and advice if you have a partner who is a sports guy.

Lil Wayne

Rapper, Singer, Songwriter, Record Executive, Entrepreneur, and Actor Lil Wayne

Wayne has been a good friend of Skip's for over 10 years. He started out as a guest on Skip's ESPN show *First Take* and now is a guest on FS1's *Undisputed*. Their friendship has grown over the years and they are best buds. Not only is Wayne one of the most talented rappers/musicians in the world today, but his IQ level is genius, and he has a special love for sports. So naturally, I needed to get his perspective on sports and relationships, and he had plenty to share.

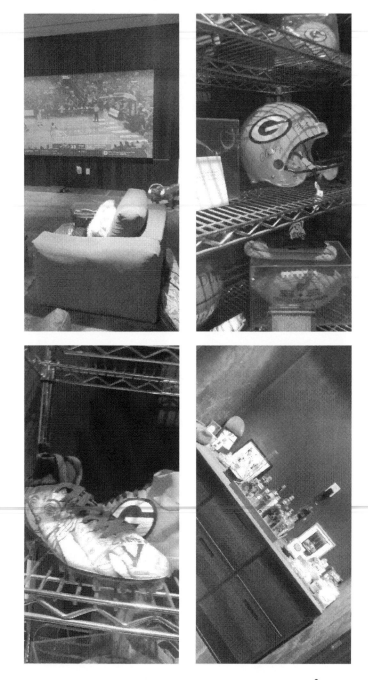

Lil Wayne sent me these photos of his
"Sports Man Cave" for my book.

Lil Wayne

"I have never had any issues with my girl over watching the game. It's usually a learning experience for her every time: to learn more about the game and me.

"There's no compromising needed, but she may disagree.

"She hates to watch a game without me.

"I have one simple rule: It's 'Go Lake show!' 'Go Sawx!' And of course, 'GO PACK, GO!' Or go to another room and watch Netflix. Simple.

"Sports will always be genuine when it's shared with the homies.

"It'll always be authentic when watched alone. It's then when you get to learn new things about the sport that'll only stand out to you when watching comfortable and by yaself. Man-cave-with-the-door-closed life!"

Billy Bob Thornton

Actor, Filmmaker, Songwriter, Musician, and Singer Billy Bob Thornton

Billy is a one-of-a-kind guy. But interesting enough, Skip and Billy are two guys with such similar backgrounds growing up, it's scary. This was discovered after Billy was a guest on Skip's show *First Take* back in 2013, when he had just published his autobiography entitled *Billy Bob Tapes: A Cave Full of Ghosts*—which, by the way, is one of the best autobiographies I have read: I highly recommend it!

Skip started reading the book after Billy was on his show, and he could not put it down. For at least two weeks straight, he would call me nightly in NYC while he was living in Connecticut, and he would provide a play by play of the latest chapter and how powerful it was. When Skip's birthday was a few weeks away, I decided the only gift that he would truly love was to have Billy show up at a dinner so they could discuss his book together. I tracked him down, and Billy, who is the most gracious person alive—in addition to being an Oscar-winning filmmaker, actor, singer, songwriter, and musician—responded, in the midst of filming a TV show out of the country.

From that moment on, Billy has not only become Skip's friend, he is also mine. He was the first person to help us transition from NYC to California with his constant generosity, love, and contact list of doctors, vets, and everyone else one needs to know when moving to a new city. He is one of the most brilliant people I know, has the best sense of humor, AND is a sports guy! His dad was a high school basketball coach, and Billy was a really good high school baseball player who even considered playing professionally for a while. But, lucky for us, acting won over! But sports is in his blood, and he is a huge fan of the St. Louis Cardinals and the Indianapolis Colts. Not only did Billy offer up his relationship advice when you are with a sports guy, but he also shared a song he wrote for his band, The Boxmasters, and it is so right on the money—mind you, he penned this song a few years ago, before I wrote this book.

Billy Bob Thornton

There is no bigger St. Louis Cardinals fan than Billy Bob Thornton. He describes himself as a rabid fan with a long list of jinxes and superstitions he strongly believes will affect the outcome of a game, such as the following:

- If the team is playing their first game out of 162 and they lose, he believes they will then lose all 162!
- When watching the Cardinals against the Brewers, he can't bear to watch if the Brewers are up to bat: he changes the channel while keeping tabs on his phone until the half-inning ends. As soon as the Cardinals are up to bat again, the game is back on. (The same goes for Cubs games—he can only watch when the Cardinals are batting.)
- He will never call or text a friend when the Cardinals are playing.
- And if his wife Connie ever says they are winning, it's the kiss of death! He will gently say, let's be humble, don't be arrogant and please don't talk about the game, that's a sure sign they will lose.
- Things can also get a little complicated when his wife, Connie, wants to watch a game with him. The problem arises when she wants to talk about daily life stuff, things that have nothing to do with the game, and she expects him to respond. His only response is "Can't this wait until the game is over in two hours? Just give me two hours, please!" He prefers watching the game with their daughter, Bella, who's following in her dad's footsteps and becoming a Cardinal fan through and through.
- Billy will never wear a Cardinals T-shirt or baseball cap during their game! He will only wear their garb when the team is not playing.
- If he can imagine the team celebrating after their game—with all of the champagne and cheering—then he knows they are going to win. If he doesn't see that image before a game, he knows they are going to lose.
- No eating "stuff" next to him during a game, like crunchy bags of chips, Doritos, pretzels, or anything that makes a loud noise!

- He needs to hear what the ref or umpire is saying. If there is a crunching sound just as the official speaks, it's no good.
- Billy is such a sports fan that his only request in his rider (a clause in an actor's contract outlining things he must have when making a movie) is DirecTV in his trailer so he can watch the games!
- He's also perfected the art of reading the scroll at the bottom of the screen and watching the game at the same time. It's worth it to make sure he never misses a second of the action!

"I'm Watching The Game"
Written by Billy Bob Thornton and JD Andrew

Stop telling me stuff, quit asking me shit
Can't you see I'm watching the game
I've had just about enough, I'm going to pinch a fit
If the Cardinals lose you'll be the one to blame

Stop rubbing my chest, stay off of my chair
For Pete's sake, it's only for two hours
The damn game's a mess, and this ump ain't fair
Why don't you go out and pick me some flowers

You know how I hate those fucking Cubs
I've told you at least a thousand times
Right now, I can't give you no damn back rub
With two out and two on in the ninth

Later on you can drive me insane
But right now, I'm watching the game

Stop telling me stuff, quit asking me shit
Can't you see I'm watching the game
I've had just about enough, I'm going to pinch a fit
If the Cards lose you'll be the one to blame

If we lose, this house will be a dark place
For at least a week or ten days
Right now, my mind is just on third base
And that bastard that was traded from the A's

Later on you can drive me insane
But right now, I'm watching the game
Right now, I'm watching the damn game

Michael Rapaport

Actor, Director, Podcast Host, Comedian, and Sports Personality Michael Rapaport

Michael is a die-hard New Yorker. I met him a few years ago when he was a guest on Skip's show *Undisputed*, and I felt an immediate connection to him since I am a New Yorker as well. We went to breakfast, and that was it: we clicked. We talked about LA vs. NYC (he is bicoastal, with homes on both coasts) and he offered up some really good advice about living in LA. The number one thing on his list? Don't become a mall head! We remained friends after that. He and Skip are friends as well, and he is a regular guest on *Undisputed*. Michael is a big basketball guy; he's played in the NBA All-Star Celebrity Weekend game and directed an ESPN *30 for 30* film about the 1970 Knicks. Needless to say, he is a card-carrying sports guy.

Michael Rapaport

"I love when my wife watches games with me. Some things she gets, some she doesn't. I don't care. It's always fun to watch together, and she's used to my emotional tantrums throughout the games."

Stephen A. Smith

Sports Television Personality, Sports Radio Host, Sports Journalist, and Actor Stephen A. Smith

Stephen is Skip's brother from another mother! That has been Skip and SAS's relationship for over 20 years. They worked together on an ESPN show called *Old School/Nu Skool* and then again on *First Take*. They are forever buddies. Needless to say, he is also my good friend. SAS is one of the most connected guys in the sports world. His sports knowledge is off the hook, and he knows more about each player then they know about themselves. Beyond sports, he has a great fashion style and sense of humor, AND he is a regular guest star on his favorite soap, *General Hospital*. He has interesting thoughts on relationships and sports and was eager to express them.

Stephen A. Smith

Turn-offs

- When the woman he is with thinks she knows more about sports than he does—and in reality, she doesn't—the fun "let's watch a game together" time turns from good to bad really fast!
- Some women are very competitive, and if they are watching a game with him, he finds that a majority of the time they try to distract him from the game to level and measure who is more important: the game or her! "If you are going to make me choose between you or the game, especially when it is a crucial moment in the game, I'm going to choose the game over you!"

Jinxes

- He will speak on the phone during a commercial, and if he is still on the phone when the game resumes, that's OK, but he will never start a call while the game is being played.
- The best thing to ever happen to sports fans was the invention of the DVR and TiVo. They allow fans to hit pause if need be and not lose the momentum. BUT, you cannot venture far away from the place you are watching the game, or you run the risk of running into someone who'll tell you what just happened or what they think is about to happen in the game. So stay close to home!
- He will never have sex during a game, especially when the Yankees, Steelers, or Knicks are playing. He has gone 0 for 20, losing 20 games in a row when giving into sex during a game! He can have sex before the game, through halftime, or after the game, but just never during!

Kevin Dillon

Actor Kevin Dillon

Kevin is the reason why Skip and I met; therefore, he holds a special place in our hearts forever. I had not spoken to or seen Kevin for 13 years, and yet when I contacted him about my book, he was as sweet as he was the first day I accompanied him to his media appearances. He really got a kick out of the fact that he was the catalyst for Skip and me meeting. He is a true New Yorker and loves his NY teams, but he also knows what it's like to be in a split-sports team household. Kevin offers up fun advice to help keep your love going, no matter what team you root for.

Kevin Dillon

Kevin Dillon and his girlfriend have the typical East-meet-West relationship. He's from New York and loves the Knicks, Giants, Rangers, and Mets. She's from LA and loves the Lakers and Rams. "We compromise, though," he says. "I show her team some love, and in return, she shows my team some love!"

But he also doesn't mind taking the time to teach her about a game or athlete when they are watching together. He says it makes it even more fun.

Vince Gill

Singer, Songwriter, and Multi-instrumentalist Vince Gill

Vince is from Norman, Oklahoma, and Skip is from Oklahoma City. Over the years, their paths have crossed; not in person, but in life situations. Vince moved from Norman to OKC as a kid, and both guys ended up going to the same high school. Recently, Skip found out he was being inducted into the Northwest Classen Hall of Fame. This is the second year they are inducting a notable, and the first inductee last year was none other than Vince Gill. Vince is a sports guy and roots for the Nashville Predators. Since Skip and I have both been huge fans of Vince's music for years, and given their ironic history together, I knew I had to include his thoughts on sports and relationships in my book. He was kind enough to agree to be included, and after chatting, I can say he is truly one of the nicest people on this planet. We had a fun conversation, and he revealed sweet and honest takes on how he and his wife— singer, songwriter, and musician Amy Grant—watch games together.

Vince Gill

Vince's team is the Nashville Predators. Normally he watches alone, but every once in a while, his wife wanders in and decides to sit down and watch with him. He has no issues with that at all. She is not a big sports fan, but he says when she finally commits, she's all in: whooping, hollering, and cheering on the team. Vince says she's a "great hang" and fun to be with. He does his best to explain to her what's happening during the game and the endless rules. In the end, they both have a good time.

He's also a big fan of the Belmont Bruins baseball and football teams. He has been a fan for years.

As far as superstitions and jinxes go, when he was younger, he believed that by turning off the TV, his team would have a better chance of winning! He has long outgrown that, but he knows plenty of guys that still swear by it.

Shannon Sharpe

Hall of Famer and Sports Personality Shannon Sharpe

Shannon played in the NFL from 1990 through 2003. In 2009, he was inducted into the NFL Hall of Fame. Soon after he retired from playing football, he became a national broadcast and radio sports analyst. He currently debates Skip daily on *Undisputed*. Shannon has fun and interesting takes.

Shannon Sharpe

Shannon believes he can better form opinions on what's happening without hearing the announcers' interpretations.

"Watching with me has always been tough because I watch every game with the sound turned down, except for the Olympics. Women in my life have tried to watch with me, but it's like, 'This isn't very entertaining without the sound.' They get bored pretty quickly.

"I've tried to take them to the games. They like the idea of that until they realize everyone wants to talk to me, and they usually get left out, and that's no fun, either. So even what they're looking forward to turns out to be not so great.

"My lifestyle is just so hard on them because of the job I do now. I have to be up by 3 a.m., and I'm not nocturnal. I can't see in the dark. I have to turn on the lights. None of this is very fun for them."

Chapter 18

Final Thoughts

If I had to sum up this book in one word, it would be "compromise." No matter your situation, that's the key to a happy relationship. Whether your guy is a doctor, lawyer, computer technician, engineer, or sports guy, it just won't work without compromise.

My mission is to help all those ladies who have no interest in sports but are dating or married to a sports-obsessed guy. I know I can't be the only female out there in this boat, so look at me as your life preserver. Again, my situation and the relationship I have with Skip and his sports obsession are 100 times larger and more extreme than what most women have with their guy, but I can relate to each and every one of you and your gripes.

There are times when every person, male or female, has to pick his or her "spot" in a romantic partnership. No one is perfect, not even you! That's the first thing you have to accept. You may think you are, but you're not. So if we're not perfect, how can you expect your guy to be?

We all have flaws and imperfections, but my father taught me a life lesson a long time ago which I still use daily. It's as simple as it gets. Whenever I would ask his opinion on a guy I was dating or a job I was thinking about leaving my current job for, his answer was always the same:

"Take a piece of paper and write on the right side the pros, and on the left side the cons. Then see which side outweighs the other. That's your answer!"

And that's exactly what I did after dating Skip for a while. The right side read like a dream. Here's a small sample:

- I was attracted to him physically.
- He has a great sense of style.
- He has a dry sense of humor. (It's different than mine, but I actually like it!)
- He is spiritual, kind, and caring.
- He likes movies. (That's a plus in my book since I adore escaping into a theater and seeing two or three films on a Saturday!)
- He eats the same way I do: clean and healthy.
- We both love walking and can rack up miles and miles wherever we are, never thinking about taking a car or cab.
- We really enjoy each other's company: just the two of us hanging out and never bored, even when doing nothing.

On the cons side, there was just one big word: SPORTS.

I sat back and stared at the paper, rewrote the lists over and over, but soon realized it was the same every time. And as you can see, the pros won!

In addition to my "determining" list, there was a moment when we were together that helped seal the deal for me: We drove out to Long Island from the city to visit my mom one weekend. She had made her incredible matzo ball soup and some of the basic Jewish food I had grown up with.

At this point, Skip and I had been together for about six months. I sat back and watched Skip—a non-Jewish guy from Oklahoma City—enjoy every last piece of the lunch my mother had placed on his plate, a new cuisine that he had never eaten before. He expressed a sincere interest in her life, who she was, what she thought. Soon after, she fell in love with him as if he was her own son. Thirteen years later, reflecting back, it brings tears to my eyes.

I knew then that he was the guy for me.

The years since then have flown by and been amazing. Have we had disagreements? Sure. Have we gotten on each other's nerves? Oh yeah. Being the stubborn people that we both are, have we had nights where we laid in bed waiting for the other to apologize for some unintended and STUPID insult? Absolutely!

But have the years together been worth all that? You bet.

Skip, for all his late-night basketball games, nail-biting Super Bowls, and Marches full of Madness, is more than that. He's the man who swept me off my feet, who charmed my mother, who never forgets a special day, who has special cards and gifts hidden for me months in advance! He's everything on the right side of the list.

If you get down to it, you'll realize (hopefully) that your man, in his own way, is the same. Write that list, but please take your time. How long is the right side? Does it start to make the sports obsession look smaller in comparison? Does it begin to make you think that maybe this guy is worth sitting next to through a game, or leaving his lucky but dirty jersey unwashed for weeks?

I sure hope so. Because when the right side fills the page and starts to fill the back, how can we resist?

Made in the
USA
Middletown, DE